Community Care
Practice Handbooks

General Editor: Martin Davies

Teaching Practical Social Work

Community Care Practice Handbooks

General Editor: Martin Davies

Teaching Practical Social Work

A Guide for Supervisors

Hazel Danbury

COMMUNITY
CARE

Gower

First published in 1979 by Bedford Square Press.

Published by

Gower Publishing Company Limited
Gower House
Croft Road
Aldershot
Hants GU11 3HR
England

Gower Publishing Company
Old Post Road
Brookfield
Vermont 05036
USA

Danbury, Hazel
 Teaching practical social work : a guide for supervisors. —
 2nd ed. — (Community care practice handbooks)
 1. Social work education — Great Britain
 I. Title   II. Series
 361'.007'1141   HV11

ISBN 0-566-05187-7

Printed in Great Britain at the
University Press, Cambridge.

Contents

Preface to the Second Edition

The practical teaching of social work can be an exciting and satisfying experience. However, new supervisors still sometimes cannot enjoy the rewards of training students because they are not well enough prepared or supported in the task. The skills of a teacher are demanded as well as those of a social worker, and it should be remembered at the outset that a good social worker does not automatically make a good teacher, nor do all social workers necessarily enjoy supervising. For those who do, however, it can enrich their own work, e.g. by keeping them abreast of new developments, ideas and ways of thinking; the supervisor is constantly re-examining his own ways of working in a constructively critical way. The current trend is for training officers to insist that social workers attend a supervisors' course before taking on a student.

This book can be used as an adjunct to such a course, as well as being a reference manual for busy social workers who have to supervise social work students with little or no preparation and training. The book aims to cover comprehensively and concisely the practical issues involved. It sets out the major problems facing the new supervisor, with suggestions for handling them. Discussion is deliberately kept to a minimum; the book may be used as it stands, or as a basis for seminars amongst groups of supervisors. It has been written with the local authority supervisor in mind, but this does not exclude its wider applicability to a variety of social work agencies.

The book focuses on the individual supervisor and student and how, within this framework, a range of social skills, methods and techniques may be taught. It does not dismiss other teaching methods, such as group and team teaching, but accepts the reality that availability of these and many other resources are very limited and restricted to a few areas. Most supervisors have to work without such aids as audio-visual equipment, in-service training programmes, specialised community and group workers. It is assumed that where these resources are available, their use will be exploited to the full.

The material is presented in such a way that it is a step-by-step guide from the point at which a social worker is asked to take a student, to the end of the placement. The subjects covered, in order, are: preparation, orientation and integration; common anxieties of supervisor and student; selection of cases; recording; methods of teaching and supervision; evaluation and aims of placement; termination.

Social workers have little time for reading and are increasingly dependent upon reference books for basic necessary information (see Davies 1985 2nd Edn). The aim of the second edition is to keep the book as a concise, practical guide to supervision, but to bring it up to date; for example, new methods of supervision are increasing in popularity, even though the traditional model of individual supervision is still the basic one. Nowadays it is used far more in conjunction with other types, for example, shared or group supervision, live supervision, audio-visual supervision. As well as benefits, these can bring additional problems — for example, who is ultimately responsible for writing the final report and, by implication, passing or failing the student?

Recording is another major subject which needs expanding in this edition, as the question crops up of open files with access to them by clients. All agencies are looking at their recording outlines, and at such questions as restriction and content of records.

For simplicity and easy reading, the generic pronoun 'he' is used.

1 Education and Training: General Considerations

Purposes of Training

Implications of generic training

There has developed considerable confusion since courses became generic and the Social Services Act 1970 came into force, as to what the social worker's role is and whether students are being equipped in their training for the work expected of them in social service departments.

Discussion of these topics is outside the scope of this book, but readers are advised to refer to the current literature where they have been comprehensively examined (see References).

Summarising, the concept of generic training implies that

> The student should have developed some ability to work with a wide range of problems and a wide range of personality.
> He should be familiar with differing psychological and sociological theories and with social work methods, for example:
>> crisis intervention; (see Rapoport 1970)
>> task or problem-centred casework; (see Reid and Epstein 1972)
>> brief/short-term casework;
>> long-term casework;
>> diagnostic, problem-solving and functional schools of social work; including Hollis's levels of casework intervention; (see Hollis 1964; Perlman 1957; Smalley 1967)
>> systems and unitary approach; (see Goldstein 1973; Pincus and Minahan 1973)
>> social group work;
>> community work.
> He also needs an ability to adapt to working in different social work agencies, to work across disciplines and to transfer learning (see Stephens 1963; Harris 1983; CCETSW 1981).
> The requirements of the newly qualified worker in

terms of generic training are indeed formidable.

Expectations of departments

Social services departments frequently have expressed the belief that students are not properly equipped to do the job when they have been trained, but it is questionable, in the light of the foregoing remarks, whether their expectations are realistic.

There is still debate as to what should be taught on courses, and what should be taught as in-service training.

Learning is unending, and it is not realistic to expect the newly qualified worker to know everything. Courses give them a basic generic training and the tools to go on learning and developing skills subsequently.

Procedural methods are more appropriately left to in-service training, as courses do not have the time or resources, and every agency differs. However, students are frequently expected to have had detailed knowledge of this sort taught on their courses. This gives rise to comments such as their not being trained for the job.

Realistic expectations would be that a student returns with a great deal of theoretical knowledge on a wide variety of academic subjects, plus a certain amount of practical experience:

> This needs backing up with in-service training on practical issues specific to the agency, in addition to training in the execution of statutory duties.
>
> Consolidation and integration continue to take place after the course has finished, as the worker gains more experience in the application of theory. Consolidation usually takes upwards of two years — a point which has great significance in view of the trend of rapid promotion away from the field, in the 1970s.
>
> There is increasing evidence for the necessity of more specialist post-qualifying courses for those who develop particular interests in specialised areas, but have not been taught the necessary skills.

An example of a college handout setting out the aims of training is given below.

Objectives of CQSW course

To provide a professional social work training for a wide

range of posts in the social services, hospitals, general practice, probation and voluntary bodies.

The aim is to prepare the students to work with individuals, families, groups and communities by activating these groups to use their own potential and that of their environment.

The methods used in the above are:

    The exploration in academic study of

        behaviour through sociological and psychological theories;

        the nature of social problems and their origins through the history and development of social policy;

        the study of law and current legislation and welfare rights;

        the study of political institutions and public finance.

    Students are taught

        an understanding of the agencies involved in delivering the services, and their roles and relationships to other institutions;

        methods of intervention — case work (crisis intervention, brief and extended case work, task centred case work, the unitary approach), group work, community work, working with volunteers, admission to residential institutions and collaboration with residential staff;

        students are taught the above in the logical sequence of study of the development of the individual from infancy to death.

        Reference should be made to CCETSW Revised Guidelines (1981).

Expectations of local authority students

Students frequently have similar expectations to those of their employing agencies. Two major complaints in their training seem to be:

        They are not trained to do child care statutory work whilst on their qualifying courses. This is particularly in regard to care and supervision orders, and child abuse. It would seem, on closer inspection, that the students may really be saying that they do not feel equipped to deal with unmotivated clients. Curiously, probation students do not appear to share this anxiety to the same extent.

Students can accept that statutory procedures may belong more appropriately to the field of in-service training. The problems of working with unmotivated clients should be given more attention both in the theoretical content of the course, e.g. in college seminars, as well as in the fieldwork teaching, where possible.

Students may feel they are not being helped to deal with the vast range of problems which will face them, when they are qualified. They accept that there has to be selection in teaching material; that it is impossible on a course to gain experience of working with every possible type and combination of problem, but they cannot help always being aware of the areas which are not being covered. This would appear to be an insoluble problem which can, perhaps, best be tackled by a slight shift in teaching/learning focus. Instead of assessing mainly in terms of problem and personality category, more emphasis could be placed on understanding, acknowledging and sharing the clients' feelings with regard to their situation. The social worker, who with awareness of the lack of resources has feelings of helplessness and futility, may at least help the client to feel that he is not totally isolated in his feelings about the position, even if no practical help can be offered to alleviate it. The client is much better able to accept the lack of resources and the fact that the social services cannot provide, for example, a telephone which is a necessary life-line, if he is aware that the social worker enters into his feelings about this. The student needs the supervisor's help in:

accepting the reality of limited resources;

accepting that he should not be expected to be omnipotent and solve all problems, dealing with the intense anxiety generated by others' expectations that he should;

allowing himself to communicate this to his client and share in the client's feelings and reactions.

Student's Expectation from and
Assessment of the Placement

A helpful exercise for both student and supervisor is for the supervisor to ask the student at the beginning of the placement to record his expectations, what he hopes to learn, what activities he would like to engage in, on what areas he feels particular concentration is needed (see below). He may also record what he expects and hopes for from the supervision sessions. Just as he is learning to clarify with his clients what their task is, so it is important to clarify the tasks with the supervisor. Differences in expectations between student and supervisor may therefore be dealt with immediately, without a build-up of frustrations and anxieties.

When the tutor makes the first visit to the agency (see chapter 2) the three of them may find it useful to discuss, review and maybe revise what the student has written; it adds a focus to this meeting, which is frequently needed.

At the end of the placement, the supervisor and student can use this as part of the evaluation process and assess how far the expectations have been fulfilled.

THINGS I HOPE TO LEARN FROM MY FIRST PLACEMENT

I see my placement as offering a challenge to my skills as a social worker on a very broad front and as well an excellent place in which to test myself out. For example, I feel that it will challenge my ability to understand the complexity of human nature, to work in a multi-disciplinary setting and more directly test my ability as a social worker. From the beginning my expectations of the placement have been high but after about 3 months at the clinic, I feel that they have been substantially confirmed. The problem with it, as with most stimulating experiences, is that the more I learn the more I am aware of what I don't know! I will detail below the areas on which I feel I need to continue to work, with an eye to my probable future as a social worker in Birmingham.

Basic social work skills. Despite increasing theoretical 'knowledge' about social work methods and over two years' experience, I feel that there is still a long way to go in developing the many basic skills of communication. I feel that I need to learn more about facilitating the client's communication, and of receiving it and some relevant and meaningful response. Specifically I find a problem in recognising verbalising back to the client in a helpful manner the emotional response aroused in me. I feel that I am only just beginning to learn to make interpretations.

Social work methods. I feel that my primary difficulty in this area is that of sharing with the client a definition of the problem and the objectives of treatment. Beyond this is the problem of carrying these through in a disciplined manner that permits realistic assessment of its value.

This placement has offered me the opportunity to develop a specialism which has always fascinated me. Moreover, I feel that it has relevance to most local authority social work cases at an indirect if not at a direct level. Firstly, it is clarifying for me the areas in which psychiatry and/or hospitalisation can help and the areas where it cannot. Secondly, to learn about diagnoses and cause of the social and medical implications of these. Also of treatment methods and concepts, many of which seem to me to be of direct value to social work. On another level, the complexities of pathological behaviour seem to be of value in understanding 'normal' behaviour and indeed in differentiating, if possible, the two. The setting enables one to work with problem behaviour directly, less fettered to other considerations than in the local authority. Moreover, it seems that it almost gives a licence to interfere and the hospital in some way to create a climate of expectations different to the usual social services office.

I find it interesting from a sociological viewpoint, in that most of the clients seem to be middle class and relatively articulate — a threatening thing in itself.

I hope that after Christmas I can participate in one of the group's activities and learn about an area in which I am still cloudy. Also to become more involved in the psychosexual clinic.

As a hospital the placement offers an opportunity to gain factual knowledge about other illnesses and something of the problems of medical social work.

Finally, there are the broader aspects of community resources. I am not particularly interested in the borough and its problems except in so far as they have similarities to national problems and implications for them.

When considering my expected return to Birmingham, it would seem more sensible that I concern myself mostly with either organisations that operate nationally or legal or administrative matters. Nevertheless I shall need to learn some things that are relevant to my clients.

In conclusion, I feel that so far this has been a valuable placement. Its major limitation – i.e. its specialisation – is also a strength. It offers an opportunity to develop skills in a specific manner from which I can later generalise rather than the other way about, which I feel is less rewarding and less efficient.

College days and placement days
The programme of most generic courses is very heavy, so it is important for the student not to feel in any conflict between the college and field demands which are made on him.

Most courses have academic and practical work running concurrently, the aim being to facilitate the integration of theory with practice. It is unhelpful for the student if he finds himself in a situation where he has to make choices between the college and the agency, e.g. if he has to miss lectures because one of his clients is in court.

It should be quite clear which days he is in college and which in the placement.

If the student misses some of the academic course, he is frequently unable to make it up, since it cannot be repeated; as the course is one of training for a profession it is unfortunate if he has gaps which may result in his being less well equipped to do his job.

Concurrent v. block placements
Some courses are not concurrent, but have block placements and whole terms in college. Problems of integrating theory and practice may be greater in these cases, where the student is not relating one to the other throughout the course, and can split them off, not seeing them as in any way related.

Many students on concurrent courses are in placement where they are practising a particular specialisation before having been taught the theory; the importance of relevant reading around the cases and contact with the tutor over this is stressed in the next chapter.

Agency meetings

Frequently the student is exposed to pressures in the agency to attend meetings. This can cause difficulties.

The student is there primarily to learn to be a skilled practitioner; if he attends too many meetings at the expense of work with clients, the balance of his training is in question.

Ideally, he should experience agency staff, team, allocation meetings, etc., but not necessarily attend all of them; case conferences could be considered an exception, as these should help to develop his assessment and planning skills.

In-service training programmes frequently cause conflicts among students if they are on college days, or during placement hours. Again, they can consume a large amount of time which is set aside for practical work. A resolution of this could be for the student, supervisor and tutor to discuss together what is valuable in the in-service training scheme and introduce it into the college academic course — e.g. guest lecturers, films.

Length of placements

Whatever the length of course, and placement, many supervisors feel that placements are too short, and though this may well be the case, without lengthening all courses it may be impossible to give more time to fieldwork days as this would be at the expense of time spent in academic work. Maximum use of the time available must be made by the student and supervisor to develop the student's skills and facilitate the integration of theory into his practical work.

It should be remembered that the practice part of training takes up a minimum of 50 per cent of a CQSW course.

2 Placement Preparation, Orientation and Management

The Decision to Supervise a Student

A social worker may be approached to take a student by his senior, the training officer or, more rarely nowadays, directly by the college tutor. In local authority social services departments which include hospitals, and the probation service, the request will have to be made through the training officer at some stage. Ideally, the supervisor should be approached several weeks before the placement is due to start; he should not have pressure put on him to accept.

It is important for a supervisor to want to teach and his promotion should not be dependent upon having supervised students, as being a good social worker does not necessarily mean that one will be a good social work teacher. As the allocation of placements is increasingly being made by specially appointed college tutors in conjunction with training officers, the supervisor will have to ensure that he knows:

from which college the student comes;

type and length of course, e.g. non-graduate two year, postgraduate one year, pre-professional, etc.;

which placement, e.g. first, second;

details and syllabus of the course, e.g. its orientation and whether it includes groupwork, community work, details of supervisors' meetings, reading lists;

times and dates of fieldwork placement;

basic information relating to the student: name, age, address, practical experience, education;

a copy of the last practical work evaluation if this is not a first placement;

guidelines to aims and expectations of the placement, evaluation outlines; other useful information to help the supervisor.

The choice of placements is obviously limited by availability. Even so, in selecting a student for a supervisor it is very important to ensure that there is a working affinity between them. The quality of supervision is more important than the type of agency. One of the major instruments in learning is the supervisory relationship. It is essential, therefore, that the supervisor and student relate to each other in such a way as to facilitate learning; it helps if they like each other; possibilities of personality clashes should be avoided. In addition, the supervisor's particular skills should be borne in mind by the tutor when arranging placements, together with the student's particular needs in terms of learning and experience. A recent trend has been for supervisors to ask to select their students. This is very understandable but it makes the tutor's job almost impossible as arrangements for placements are frequently being made up to six months ahead for a group of students. With supervisors taking a greater part in selection, the time involved in arranging placements would automatically be extended; it remains more practical for a tutor who knows both supervisor and student to do the initial 'matching', with the supervisor and student meeting to confirm this. There is then still room for change if the supervisor feels it would be impossible to work with a particular student, and vice versa.

If the question of 'matching' student to supervisor is left entirely to the supervisors, tutors become anxious in case students with known problems cannot be placed.

The supervisor should be allowed to decide what type of student he wishes to take, and from which course. The particular personality and skills of the supervisor and student should be known by the tutor and these should take priority in placing.

The tutor and supervisor should meet before the placement begins to create a common aim in terms of expectations of each other and the course as a whole; the teaching/learning team of tutor, supervisor and student is thus established at the outset. The supervisor also needs to know when the tutor will be visiting the agency (ideally at least twice) as well as the availability of the tutor outside the formal meeting times, e.g. for crisis purposes. He will also need to know dates of supervisors' meetings at the college.

As first placements have to be arranged by the college several months before the beginning of the course, it is usually impractical and impossible for the student to have much say in the choice of supervisor or agency; this has to be left to the discretion of the tutor who has wider knowledge of the total situation.

Fitting a student into the agency
Ideally, if the agency committed to student supervision accepts the idea of students being a permanent feature of the office, then the supervisor's caseload is lessened in order to allow time for preparation, reading, weekly supervision, meetings with the tutor and college, etc.

Provision of accommodation is necessary; this may be anything extending from a chair in a corner with access to a desk and telephone, to a room especially set aside for students.

Provision of support systems is helpful, e.g. relevant literature; social workers to advise in the supervisor's absence, etc.

Preliminary meeting Whenever possible, the supervisor and student should meet before the start of the placement, with or without the tutor. This initial meeting helps the student to feel familiar with the agency; he has a more realistic idea of the setting in which he will work. He can discuss the area of work in which he needs help, and the supervisor is better able, in conjunction with the knowledge given by the tutor, to assess his learning needs and select cases more appropriately. Such a meeting can dispel considerable anxiety on both sides and free the student to start learning the moment his placement begins.

Contracts Either at the preliminary meeting, or during the first week of the placement, it is useful if the supervisor and student can work out some form of contract. This should not be so rigid as not to allow for flexibility, but it can provide a useful framework and reference point for the placement.

Two examples of contracts follow, one from a placement in an area team, the other in a hospital.

FRAMEWORK FOR FIELDWORK PLACEMENTS
CONTRACTS

1 Practical arrangements

days of and length of placement
student's use of desk, telephone, secretarial facilities
time student expected to arrive and leave
reading time
attendance at agency meetings, e.g. team, allocation.

2 Supervision

priority of supervision time
recordings in to supervisor in time to read before
day and time and length of regular supervision
type of supervision

3 Recording

for agency and supervision

4 Work load

type, range and number of cases
other related activities
other areas for student learning

5 Duty

student's observation and/or participation

6 Three-way meetings with college tutor

7 Procedure if problems arise

8 Evaluation

9 Overall aims of the placement:

supervisor's aims; student's aims

PLACEMENT CONTRACT

First fieldwork placement in L.B. Thamesford between student, Fiona Smith, and supervisor.

1.   *Practical arrangements*
(a) Placement is three days a week, Monday, Tuesday, Wednesday, from January to June.
(b) Fiona Smith expected to be in agency from 9.30 a.m.– 5.00 p.m.
(c) She will have the use of a desk, telephone, secretarial and team clerk facilities.

(d) Time will be made available for her to do reading appropriate to her practical work.

(e) She will be expected to attend some area, team and allocation meetings.

2. *Supervision*

(a) Priority will be given to supervision time, which will be a minimum of 1½ hours a week, the regular day and time to be fixed.

(b) Recordings should be handed to the supervisor in time for the supervisor to have read them and written comments before the supervision time.

(c) Models and types of supervision to be flexible, e.g. joint supervision if Fiona Smith is doing work with another student.

(d) Emphasis should be placed on the integration of theory with practice, linking college and placement work, and with the transfer of learning.

(e) Another social worker to be named as the person to refer to in the supervisor's absence.

3. *Recording*

(a) Fiona Smith should keep her agency files up to date and record in the accepted agency way: she should remain aware of the policy of client access to records.

(b) Recording for supervision — e.g. process recording — should be handed to the supervisor well before supervision.

(c) If possible and/or appropriate, she should have some experience in writing reports for court, and/or social histories.

4. *Work load*

(a) The work load should be limited so that there is plenty of time for discussion and reflection.

(b) Ideally, Fiona should be able to experience the whole range of types of work in an area team. As her experience has been in child care, it is important for her to have some family work, but also work with the elderly, sick and handicapped in order to broaden her knowledge and experience.

(c)   Other related activities: this should be left flexible.
(d)   Other areas of student learning: ditto.

5.   *Duty*

Towards the middle of the placement, Fiona should spend some time observing duty; later on she may participate in it.

6.   *Three-way meetings* with the college tutor should be prepared for by all parties. The tutor will be given a résumé of the work done before the meeting, and all three should have some ideas of areas for discussion. The placement contract and assessment guidelines will be referred to at these meetings.

7.   *Procedure* if problems arise is that the tutor should be contacted and possible extra three-way meetings arranged.

8.   *Evaluation*

(a)   The evaluation is continuous throughout the placement.
(b)   The report will be discussed by the student and supervisor before being written.
(c)   The student and supervisor will sign the finished report prior to its being sent to the college tutor. The student will be able to add comments if she feels it necessary.

9.   *Overall aims of the placement*

(a)   Student's aims:
Apart from the above, to gain a generic experience of work in a typical inner city social services area team.
(b)   Supervisor's aims:
To provide the above.

Signed   Supervisor..............................

Student.................................

Date   ....

STUDENT PLACEMENT, SOCIAL WORK DEPARTMENT, Y HOSPITAL

FINAL PLACEMENT: October—May, 3 days a week

Aims

1. To gain an understanding of the function of a social work department in a psychiatric hospital.
2. To broaden understanding and knowledge of services available in the mental health field.
3. To develop awareness of the relationship of theory to practice in this setting, including comparison of different models.
4. To take work appropriate to fulfilling the objectives below.

Objectives

1. To understand and utilise the relationship between the social work department and other disciplines.
2. To examine and engage in the relationship between the hospital social work team and area based social work teams.
3. To examine and engage in the relationship between the hospital social work team and other agencies.
4. To gain greater understanding of mental illness/health and of possible treatments available both within the hospital and outside.
5. That the above be related to the legislative framework.
6. To understand the role of the individual social worker based on a ward and specifically the relationship between the social worker and the ward based staff.
7. Within the ward base to work with groups there
   (a) to understand the value of group work in this context.
   (b) to develop a greater understanding of group processes/dynamics.
   (c) to see how different disciplines fit into the group process.
   (d) to develop personal skills in this area.
8. To work with a representative mixture of individual clients primarily from the ward base but to include work from other areas as well, e.g. elderly, outpatients.

9. To be aware of the importance of work in the community including participation in the home assessment service, its concomitants and after-care. Develop skills in these areas.
10. To consider the appropriateness of different types of intervention and experience these where possible.
11. To have contact with and/or visit those agencies which relate to the development of the placement.

Context
The primary base of the placement will be with the social work team relating to the ward and its catchment area.

It is recognised that a day-to-day working relationship will be necessary with the members of the social work team working in the ward, especially the team leader and that there will be some role blurring of the supervisory process between these people and the supervisor. In view of this it is agreed that student, supervisor and the team leader concerned, should meet together at least once a month to discuss progress.

Supervision will take place weekly with reports available beforehand when possible. It is recognised that the two days in college will set certain limits to the placement. Where possible tape recording and audio-visual equipment will be used.

We agree that the assessment will be worked on jointly while noting it ultimately remains the supervisor's responsibility. It is agreed that we have at least one interim review.

Preparation for the Student's Arrival
Organise where the student will sit. There may be no choice but if there is it is necessary to be aware that some students feel cut off from the team if they are in a room on their own; others feel unable to work quietly if they are in an open office with other social workers.

Ensure the team knows: that the student is coming, when, and which days; where his desk is; that other social workers' help may be sought in looking for suitable cases.
Cases: Select approximately two cases before the student arrives. These should be chosen after discussion with the tutor as being the most appropriate teaching material. Selection of cases is dealt with in more detail in chapter 4.

Reading relevant to the specific cases should be made available, e.g. in a psychiatric setting the student may need to read about specific mental disorders in order to work with his clients; he may not have his theoretical psychiatric lectures until later in the course.

Making the Student Welcome

The importance to the student of the supervisor's contacting him, even if only by a welcoming letter, is often overlooked by both tutors and supervisors.

Example: A student beginning her final placement commented: 'My new supervisor wrote to me; I felt as if they really wanted me and were planning for me to come. In my last placement I just turned up, hoping I was expected, only to find my supervisor not in that day.' She said she had felt in the way on her first placement, but in the last one stated that she felt she had a right to be there and a right to her supervisor's time.

Some supervisors consider that students who are welcomed in this way are over-protected and made too dependent; it is also argued that the stress to which a student, who is not welcomed, is exposed, is useful for both supervisor and student in teaching both of them how the student copes with stress situations.

Some arguments against this are:

It does not help the immediate establishment of a good trusting working relationship:

The anxiety produced in the student is inappropriate anxiety, being so high as to inhibit learning, and therefore

the student is not freed to make maximum learning use of the placement from the beginning.

Whether or not a preliminary meeting is arranged, the student has a right to know what time to arrive and where to go.

Orientation of the Student

Student's arrival: It is important for the supervisor to have arrived before the student on the first day, to welcome him. If, for some reason, this is not possible, arrangements should be made for someone else to welcome the student.

Introductory session: The following areas need to be covered at some time during the introductory sessions:

What to call the supervisor. It can be very embarrassing for the student if this is not clarified at the outset and really can become a problem now that most social workers are on Christian name terms with each other, as the student may be unsure how to address his supervisor.

Show the student around the building so that he knows which room he is to be in, where to put his things, where to eat, etc.

Introduce the student to other members of staff, social work, administrative, clerical, etc.

Explain administrative procedures.

Give the student the prepared folder and discuss it with him.

Explain who to go to in the supervisor's absence and introduce the student as soon as possible to these workers. Their willingness to be approached for advice should be confirmed at the introduction.

Give him details of the weekly supervision session; it is important to emphasise that this takes priority over other activities of both student and supervisor. The supervisor's accessibility at other times also needs to be clarified beforehand.

With a student on a professional course, discussion and briefing on the selected cases can take place immediately as the student is likely to be ready to start seeing clients; the longer any contact is delayed, the more anxious he may become. Students are usually very conscious of how short the course is and feel a pressure to start work immediately. The supervisor will also be able to use this time to assess further where the student is in terms of knowledge, skills, and experience.

Any relevant additional reading may be given to the student at this point.

Types and methods of recording required should also be discussed.

The student should be asked if there is anything else he wishes to know which may have been omitted. Explain to him that he is not expected to remember everything he has been told, immediately. Students sometimes need help in feeling free to ask the same question more than once, particularly if they have anxieties about becoming students again.

Information folder: It is very useful to have a file prepared for the student containing essential information. This could include:

- A map of the area covered by the agency.
- A description of the agency — its functions and limits, relevant policies, etc.

  Information about social workers and administrative staff, with names and positions, particularly those who are likely to be in contact with the student.
- A list of telephone numbers.

  Whom to go to for advice in the supervisor's absence, particularly if the supervisor is not in the same office as the student.

  The demographic structure of the area with specific social problems associated with particular parts of the area.

  A list of other agencies and resources in the area.

  Any further information thought to be necessary.

Timetable: Plan the student's timetable for about the first two days in the placement. This is to avoid the possibility of being faced with a student and not knowing how to occupy him. The anxiety may be picked up by the student and this does not help the establishment of a confident teaching/learning relationship. The student should be made to feel expected and welcomed, not an intruder.

It should be made clear to the student what time he is expected in each morning, whether or not he will be expected to do any evening visits and, if so, approximately how often.

Orientation usually takes place during the first two weeks of the placement (Butler and Elliott 1985).

The pre-professional student: So far, the discussion has centred mainly around the orientation of a professional student. However, many supervisors have a pre-professional student initially. These students tend to need more help in orientation as the social work field is frequently more unfamiliar to them.

The pre-professional student needs a placement which will introduce him to the practical field of social work.

He will need visits of observation to other agencies and services together with teaching of basic social work skills, e.g. how to interview; principles of social work; terminology and definitions; agency structures.

He may need a few days walking around the area to familiarise himself with it. It is important for the supervisor to remember that the pre-professional student is on a social administration course and is likely to have had little or no teaching in social work theory or practice. He probably will need help with his feelings of complete inadequacy.

The Importance of the Tutor/Supervisor Relationship
The tutor will be seeing the student in college, both individually and in the seminar groups, so that he should know what the student is doing in the agency. It is important for the responsibility to be shared, with the tutor and supervisor checking that each is aware of what the other is teaching.

In many very large courses, the onus may be on the supervisor to contact the tutor, who has to have overall responsibility for so many students that it is virtually impossible to have detailed knowledge of any individual one without the supervisor's more active help; this situation has potentially many problems, one of them being the making of integration more difficult for the student. There should be easy access between field and college tutor. The supervisor should feel free to ask the student what he has been doing in college during the current week. He will know what has already been covered in the academic teaching, as he should have received the term's syllabus, reading lists and course outline.

The tutor's visit to the agency
The college tutor should visit the student and supervisor in the agency to discuss the work there; in this way he can help the student to relate what he is doing in college to what he is doing in the field. Some new supervisors may feel anxious and threatened by the tutor's visit; they may feel that their ability to teach is being evaluated critically by the college. If the student has similar feelings, there is a danger of their teaming up together in hostility to the tutor and college.

That this sort of splitting is unhelpful to everybody concerned is obvious. Supervisors are more likely to feel this way if
they are unsupported by the college, and if they think that
the tutor is not interested in their problems or in what they
are teaching the students.

A meeting of three people in this sort of situation is in-
evitably difficult unless a solid relationship has been built
up, at least between tutor and supervisor, so that each is
confident about the part he is playing in the overall teaching
team. This is why it is infinitely easier if the tutor and supervisor know each other well, having worked together before.
They have clear ideas of each other's expectations and ways
of working, and can present their teaching to the student in
a more integrated form. The student will feel more comfortable if his tutor and supervisor are relaxed and easy with
each other. They will then be better able to deal with his
anxieties at being evaluated jointly by them.

As well as helping the student to integrate, and the supervisor to be in touch with college teaching, the visit is also
useful, together with the supervisors' meetings (see next
section) in giving the supervisor some yardstick against which
to measure his student's performance in relation to the rest
of the course. The tutor may also draw on the student's
practical material for generalised teaching in college seminars.
As the tutor visits a number of students, discussing their
practical work individually, he is in a position to discover
where common problems, thought to be isolated and individual, may occur; he can then plan seminars around these
topics. An example of this could be when several students
may be experiencing anxieties in regard to working with
highly articulate, intelligent clients, where their skills are
questioned. The importance of the tutor's visits cannot be
stressed enough. If tutors do not visit, the supervisor feels
that he is working in isolation; his teaching contribution
appears to be considered as unimportant by the college; he
gains the impression that the college puts small emphasis on
practical teaching, it being merely a necessary part of the
course; he cannot help the student integrate if he is not in
close touch with what is being taught in college; he certainly
does not feel himself to be a vital part of the teaching team,
but on the contrary, feels diminished and his skills devalued.

As the tutor has an overall knowledge of the student's

work, past and present, he is in a good position to indicate general areas where there may be need for extra focusing, just as the supervisor is more in touch with specific areas.

Frequency of visits. This depends largely on the length of the placement. Ideally, there should be a visit before the placement starts, unless the tutor and supervisor know each other very well, in which case the preliminary discussion may take place by telephone. This is:
> to see if the supervisor and college can work together;
> to assess the likelihood of the student's and supervisor's being able to work together;
> to see if the agency is acceptable;
> to see if there is adequate teaching material available.

At least one visit should be made, if it is a short placement; at least two, if it is a long one, for example, the whole academic session. Whereas the first visit may be used to focus on the student's expectations of the placement (see chapter 2 above), the second one, made about two-thirds of the way through the placement, can be used for a verbal mid-placement evaluation. There is then still time for work to be done on the weaker areas.

Supervisors' meetings
These vary enormously between courses. The main purpose is:
> to enable the supervisors to feel part of the teaching team;
> to share common problems in teaching, but not to discuss individual students, the place for this being between the supervisor, tutor and the student concerned;
> to be aware of what is being taught in college at a particular time, as well as what has been taught and is to be taught;
> to share discussion of new developments in the field which are relevant to training;
> to discuss any specific learning problems thrown up by the student group;
> to help the supervisor in teaching the application of theory.

The regularity of supervisors' meetings varies considerably;

they may be anything between fortnightly and once a term.

The content of the meetings also covers a wide range of topics. As well as those listed above, supervisors like to be kept informed of new developments in research and academic thinking, as well as being able to use the meetings for learning to develop their teaching skills.

Some courses encourage student participation in supervisors' meetings; others, while accepting that students should come to some if there is a specific reason, believe that supervisors have a right to meet without the students; they have their needs separately from the students. It would be difficult to use the meetings in the ways listed above, if students were to attend all their meetings; this could be at the expense of the students' own integration.

However, on those occasions when meetings include students, supervisors and tutors, the following procedure can be very fruitful; after an initial period of informal socialising, discussion groups may be formed, each group having a mixture of tutors, supervisors and students, but with none of them having their own other two parts — e.g. no tutor has any of his/her own supervisors or students in the group; similarly with the supervisors and students. They feel less constrained with this arrangement and therefore they can share ideas and experiences with as wide a variety of other people as possible. Both students and supervisors have reported back the value of these meetings, particularly in helping them to feel a commonality between them, to have baselines and to explode fantasies. A general feedback session can conclude the meeting. Perennial topics for discussion include evaluation and recording.

3 Some Common Anxieties of Supervisors and Students

The Supervisor

Relationship with the agency

The supervisor carries a dual responsibility; he is responsible to his agency and also to the college using the agency for practical teaching.

In an agency not fully committed to taking students or to understanding the amount of work and time involved in having a student, the supervisor may have conflicts about how his own caseload will suffer, particularly if his work load has not been reduced. This may lead to resentment.

Where caseloads and other work are reduced, the supervisor may be seen by colleagues who do not appreciate the time, effort and skills involved as having a 'soft option'. Arguments not to reduce his caseload may be based on the misconception that the extra work involved is limited only to the time given to weekly supervision.

Possibly the new supervisor's colleagues will see him as having changed his role, and no longer treat him as a peer. If this happens, it leads to feelings of isolation and alienation from the team.

He will have to look objectively at his agency and be able to discuss it constructively with the student. This will lead to self-questioning, not only about the agency, but the whole philosophy and ethics behind social work itself. This can be very uncomfortable (see Butrym 1976).

Relationship with the college

In order not to be a biased teacher, the supervisor will have to bring back to mind much of the social work theory which he may have rejected and examine the reasons for the rejection, in addition to examining critically the theories which he does use.

However close a relationship of teamwork may be felt to exist between college tutor and supervisor, the latter may still have anxieties about his teaching ability, knowledge and skills, and have fears about these being evaluated by the college. In some cases this can lead, if unrecognised, to a splitting of the college from the field, with the supervisor identifying with the student in seeing both of them as being evaluated by the college. The tutor's visits to the agency (discussed at greater length in chapter 2) may either resolve or exacerbate the situation depending upon how it is handled. The supervisor needs reassurance and support from the college and tutor; he also needs to know that easy access and communication between him and the college really do exist, in order to make real to him the fact that he is part of the teaching team.

Sometimes feelings of rivalry occur between the tutor and supervisor, particularly in the areas of overlap in their roles. Again, clarification and open discussion between them may resolve these. Situations like this need to be discussed by the tutor and supervisor without the student being there. Many social work teachers, both theoretical and practical, believe that the student cannot tolerate their excluding him from any contact; if this principle is rigidly adhered to, these problems may remain unresolved.

As the student and tutor have a right to meet alone together, and also the student and supervisor, so too do the tutor and supervisor have an equal right.

Some colleges give out little information and have minimal contact with the supervisor. In this situation, the supervisor can feel isolated, his contribution to training seen to be unimportant, and he may feel unsupported in any difficulties which might arise during the course of the placement (a sad situation, if he is also feeling isolated from his colleagues). In such an instance, the initiative is left entirely to the supervisor to communicate with the college. As well as causing considerable unnecessary anxiety to the supervisor and student, this attitude:

> devalues the extremely important part played by fieldwork teaching;
>
> encourages non-integration by the student of theory with practice, work in college being seen as unrelated to that in the field; and
>
> makes the already demanding task of the supervisor even greater, as he may be unaware of the content of the academic curriculum and therefore cannot school his practical teaching to fit in appropriately.

Relationship with the student
Old conflicts in the supervisor surrounding the teaching/
learning situation may be re-awakened; a good, bad or in-
different experience of supervision is likely to colour the new
supervisor's relationship with the student. Though the supervisor may be competent in handling feelings evoked in him
by the client which are inappropriate to the relationship, he
may be uneasy in experiencing them in the relationship with
his student.

Similarly, he will have to be aware of the reactions the
student has to him, and learn how to help the student handle
them.

If these feelings go unrecognised, it can impede the student's learning and professional development.

Related to the above problems is that of the boundaries of
the supervisor/student relationship:

> How much of himself should the supervisor give to the
> student?
> Where is the boundary between teacher/colleague/
> friend?
> How far should the supervisor go in using casework
> techniques in supervision if the student has a personal
> problem which inhibits his working effectively with
> clients? This is such a sensitive area, that the new super-
> visor may feel inhibited in helping the student to
> develop his skills for fear of turning the teaching rela-
> tionship into a client/worker one, even though the use
> of such techniques may seem appropriate in a particular
> instance.

It is certainly appropriate for the supervisor to clarify the
problem area with the student, pointing out how it is affecting his work with the client. If the student needs further
help, they may work out between them the means, e.g.
whether to refer him to a counsellor or psychotherapist or
whether the student wants the supervisor to help.

Students may progress, regress or not appear to move at
all; in the last two situations the supervisor may feel that he
is responsible as he is not an experienced or effective teacher.

Sometimes a student may display a difficulty which re-
flects the same one, unresolved, in the supervisor, who becomes unable to help the student. If this cannot be resolved
in the agency, the college tutor may be able to help.

Resolution of the supervisor's anxieties
These anxieties and difficulties can all be reduced once they
are openly acknowledged and discussed by the tutor and
supervisor, and the student where appropriate. Easy communication and support between college and supervisor is
essential if the teaching team is to be effective.

The Student

Role change and expectations of the course
The change of role into that of a social work student automatically creates anxieties. Some of these may include:

Regression to an earlier stage of development, especially
when the student has already held a responsible job.

Dependence, particularly upon the supervisor.

Introspection, because of the academic content of the
course, and because of the fact that use of oneself is the
major tool in the social work relationship.

Insecurity, for a number of reasons, for example,

the knowledge that his work is being continuously
assessed;

the questioning of previous patterns of work;

uncertainty about what he is being trained for;

anxiety about the 'social work mystique'.

A small caseload forces the student to examine closely
what he is doing; he can no longer be tempted to retreat
into being busy and is faced with looking at the
question of activity versus performance.

Uncertainties may exist about being able to manage the
academic content of the course, particularly in a very
mature student or any student who has been away from
the academic field for a considerable time.

Resistance to learning due to some emotional factor(s).
He may have fears of being 'analysed' and expected to
reveal his inner self, though at the same time desiring
greater self-knowledge; he is likely to feel vulnerable.

He may also have unreal expectations of himself, the
course, and what social work is.

He may come to the course with his enthusiasm about
learning overlayed with depression at the enormity of
social problems.

It is helpful if the supervisor can acknowledge these

anxieties, and let him know what he can do immediately, so that the inappropriate anxiety is dealt with, and the student freed to make use of the placement from its beginning (see chapter 2).

The student in the agency
He may feel helpless and inadequate, partly due to regression but also because of the reality of his clients' situation.

He may feel wary of intervening when a client appears to be functioning reasonably well, for fear his probing may highlight more intractable problems.

The student frequently notices a loss of spontaneity in himself; this is due to his increased self-awareness together with his endeavours to put into practice various techniques which still feel alien to him. In addition to these factors, he has to remember the whole of the interview in order to make a detailed recording of it for supervision (see chapter 6).

At some stage during the course, possibly about halfway, he is likely to experience some depression. This is frequently characterised by a sense of futility, as his awareness of the problems in social work and his intellectual understanding of them exceeds his professional ability; he has a knowledge of various methods of intervention, but has not always the skills to implement them at the appropriate times. He may set himself unattainable standards of performance, and find these impossible to reconcile with inadequate resources, conflicts between social workers and other agencies.

He may, in addition, have conflicts surrounding social work values (see Butrym 1976).

Relationship with the Supervisor
There are likely to be anxieties about how the student will get on with his supervisor, as well as his tutor. He will probably use the supervisor as a model. His attitudes and approach generally are likely to be influenced by those of the supervisor.

Transference problems
As was mentioned earlier, transference feelings towards the supervisor may cause the student great anxiety; he needs help in understanding and using them appropriately.

The student needs to know that his supervisor gives

priority to the weekly supervision session; he may feel a nuisance, an imposition, or alternatively angry and resentful if there is not a fixed weekly time set aside. Some supervisors do not have regular sessions and the effect on the student is to increase his negative fantasies and feelings, and sense of insecurity; he assumes that he ranks lowest in importance to his supervisor, and may question his right to be there. Postponements and interruptions of a regular session are also likely to have similar effects on the student.

He needs to know whether he may approach his supervisor between sessions, and to whom to go for advice in a crisis, should his supervisor not be there. He may need help in containing his anxieties until the supervision time.

The student will probably have worries about what is expected of him by his supervisor, and whether his work is of an adequate standard.

Anxieties will also be felt if he receives only praise or only negative criticism; he needs accurate continuous assessment.

If problems do occur in the placement, the student wants these clarified and dealt with as soon as possible and if necessary an extra meeting with the tutor will have to be arranged.

The student may experience some uncertainty about the relationship between himself, his supervisor and his tutor. He may have suspicions and anxieties about what happens if the tutor and supervisor have contacts which exclude him (see above).

When in difficulties, the student may be tempted to play his supervisor and tutor off against each other.

Supervising more than one student

Extra problems can occur in this situation where the student is exposed to all the feelings of sibling rivalry; he is likely to be acutely aware of all contacts between the other students and the supervisor, jealously watching to see that no student has extra attention. If the students come from different courses, rivalry between courses and tutors may come into the picture. Student units are usually geared to deal with these problems which can be very unnerving to the inexperienced supervisor.

As with all the other problems, open acknowledgement and discussion can do much to alleviate the anxieties.

Because of the individual nature of the personalities involved, it is difficult to suggest more specific ways of dealing with problems developing between supervisor and student, other than that of having open three-way discussions with the college tutor and working out possible solutions.

Student units

In agencies with student units, or in any agency which takes students from more than one course, anxieties may arise in relation to the differing nature and content of the courses. For example, there may be envious feelings if some students think they are not being taught such interesting subjects as others. It is helpful if a student discussion group can be organised whereby these problems may be aired openly.

Other difficulties may be related to the time at which the placement starts; a student beginning in January may feel inadequate beside those starting the previous October; also, it may be difficult for such a student to become part of the student group. Similar feelings of inadequacy may occur with a first placement student in relation to final placement students. Again, open discussion can help to deal with these problems. Problems of rivalry may occur between students who have the same supervisor. Once again, open acknowledgement helps to resolve these.

4 Selecting Cases

Aims in Selection
In selecting case material, the supervisor needs to keep in mind the course expectations of the particular placement (see chapter 7). It is useful to know the content of the theoretical teaching being given in college, but it is somewhat idealistic to hope to provide cases which will fit in with this; hence the necessity for providing appropriate reading material, if necessary, with the tutor's help (see chapter 2).

The supervisor should have some idea of where the student is in terms of knowledge and experience. This may have been discussed with the student and/or tutor, but if that has not been possible, at least the details of previous work experience will provide a background of information to guide the supervisor in selecting teaching material.

The cases selected before the student's arrival will provide a basis for assessment of the student's knowledge, skills and abilities, as well as indicating areas needing further concentration.

What Constitutes a Good Teaching Case
The supervisor needs to keep in mind the question of what the student can learn from a particular case in the time given. The student is there to learn:

How to assess a situation.

How to decide with the client(s) on the area of focus.

How and why to apply specific methods of social work, e.g.

individual, group or community work;

crisis intervention, problem centred, brief or extended intervention;

appropriate application of different psychological theories such as learning or psychoanalytic theories; the skills to implement the above. If the college is teaching the theories, the fieldwork teacher is training the student in the practical application of these (see chapter 2).

Ideally, the student should have the experience of initiating and completing a piece of work.

Such a case would be:

> a new referral, opened and closed during the time of the placement, so that the student develops skills of assessment, intervention and dealing with planned termination.

This does not deny the importance to the student of learning how to deal with transfer problems by taking on cases from other social workers, and in handing over clients to other workers at the end of his placement (see chapter 8); these should also be included somewhere in his practical experience as the student must learn to deal with the feelings in the client occasioned by a change of worker.

At least one case, particularly in the first placement, should be capable of some movement, in order to avoid the student's becoming too anxious and depressed with a sense of lack of achievement.

The student should also have a case where weekly interviews are necessary, to enable him to learn to use the relationship as a tool in casework, as well as to handle feelings of dependency, the transference situation, etc.

Size of Student Caseload

Some supervisors argue in favour of giving the student a large caseload in order to teach him how to work under extreme pressure. The argument against this is that being a student on a professional course is, perhaps, one of the few times in a social worker's career when he is allowed time in the placement to think about what he is doing and why; to plan his work; to examine his achievements and failures; to experiment with different social work methods in the light of his assessments.

He will then be more likely to work in a more disciplined, effective way under pressure in the future.

The number of cases a student has should be limited, building up approximately to six in the first fieldwork placement and to about ten in the final placement. This is to protect the student from being over-burdened by the agency, and to enable him to have enough time to think deeply about his work. This is of course very much dependent upon the particular student, type of agency and the student's learning needs.

The amount of interviewing time per day needs to be restricted. Early in training, more time is given to process recording (see chapters 5 and 6), thinking and discussion in supervision; towards the end of training, the student is able to spend more time interviewing and less in detailed recording. A maximum of two interviews per day seems to be the norm in the first placement.

Composition of Student's Caseload
The demands of generic training are such that the social worker should be able to deal with any problem, in either sex, any age group and setting. This makes the task of selection of cases almost impossible as it is unrealistic to expect that the student will have had experience in all areas at the end of his training (Butrym 1976).

The social work spectrum
Cases selected should be such that the student has experience in dealing with problems at each end of the social work spectrum, from almost purely practical intervention at the one extreme, to near-psychotherapeutic at the other; many students like to have a practical problem as a way into the family, and find it very difficult to establish a working relationship in situations where practical intervention is inappropriate, as for example, in many mental health cases. It is useful for the student to have such cases whilst training.

Social work methods
In addition to being able to work at different levels the student needs experience in different social work methods, for example, short-term casework, task-centred casework, the unitary model, and long-term casework. Indeed, long-term casework, which used to be the focus of practical training, now has to be included specifically, as many departments' resources are concentrated on less protracted methods. Thus, the student may easily find himself qualified with little or no experience in this area.

Age span
The age span from birth to death should be covered. Social workers may not be familiar with the normal development of

the infant and young child, and somewhere in the training a student should learn to recognise normal child development, particularly if he is to become experienced in detecting abnormal situations including child abuse. He should also be at ease with the problems of the elderly, particularly bereavement, grief and mourning, in addition to being aware of the crisis points in the life cycle, e.g. marriage, birth of a child, retirement and possible associated problems in both sexes.

Range of problems
Although it may be impossible in one placement to cover the whole range of problems likely to be referred to a social services department, an attempt should be made to allow the student to have experience of as many as possible. Problems need not necessarily be categorised in the orthodox way, e.g. psychiatric, medical, children (family), though the tendency still to do so is partly governed by the fact that in spite of recent legislation, social services are still also operating under these older separate bodies of legislation. Problems are increasingly being categorised in different ways, which may allow them to be seen in the light of their wider social and community network as well as from the aspect of the individual and family. The unitary approach to social work facilitates this way of looking at and working with multifarious problems (see Barclay Report 1982).

Student avoidance
It is natural for students to be less interested in some areas of the work, but if generic training is to be realistic the supervisor needs to be aware of why the student may be avoiding certain areas. If the social worker is ultimately likely to be exposed in his work to situations he finds unpleasant, then this should be examined and dealt with during his placement. For example, some hospital based social workers express the opinion that theirs should only be a final placement; however, others think that students should be made to face and work with the unpleasant realities of sickness and death at an early stage.

Conjoint work
This type of case is being selected more often; though it is always exciting and interesting for the student to do conjoint

work, whether marital or family therapy, it usually causes undue anxieties unless it is done towards the end of the course, as the skills demanded are considerable, and the theory usually is given at a later stage in the course.

Intake

Some supervisors favour giving the student intake and short-term work. This is very useful training when the student has reached the stage of being able to make assessments. He can only do this effectively when he has a solid theoretical foundation. Thus, in the earlier stages of the first placement it can cause great anxiety as accurate assessments demand the highest skills of the social worker. The student must feel some degree of confidence in his ability to make assessments and plan methods of intervention before he is competent to be placed in intake.

Accusations have been made that students are 'over-educated' on professional courses. However, if they do not learn the elements of social work skills on the course, they are unlikely to have the time or opportunity later. More important, perhaps, is the fact that the ability to work in the ways indicated above increases the ability to make rapid assessments and develop other techniques of working.

In selecting cases, it must be borne in mind that the problems should ideally be capable of containment when the student is not there.

It is helpful for students to be included in discussion of the allocation of cases to them. This helps them to be aware of areas of their own avoidance, highlights possible gaps in their experience and prepares them for the problems of allocation which they will have to face when trained.

Some Problems in Selection

The supervisor may have to withstand pressure from colleagues to 'off-load rubbish' under the guise of its being useful teaching material; often heard in justification is the comment 'he must be able to assess for aids and gadgets as well as deal with people's emotional problems'. All too often the student has been doing just that before coming on the course, if he has had previous fieldwork experience. Social workers in hospital have always had difficulties in selecting cases which have some continuity, and they have the additional problem of possible discharge of a patient when the student is not there. The supervisor may have selected ideal cases before the student arrives, only to find that they cannot wait and social work intervention is necessary at an earlier date.

At the time when the cases are needed, no good teaching material may be available in spite of a surfeit of referrals to the agency.

Cases may collapse, though they appeared to be suitable initially. Situations such as these can cause anxiety to both supervisor and student, each of whom feels the pressure of time, with little being achieved and each feeling responsible for 'losing' the clients.

Discussion with the college tutor can be very helpful at such times, even if it does little other than acknowledge and share the anxiety.

The supervisor must be aware of the clients' needs in selecting cases for students. The client may have already had a succession of workers. He may benefit from a student worker on two counts:

> The student may be in the agency and involved with the client for a longer period of time than another social worker; this is due to staff turnover and scarce resources. The student has far more time to devote to the client, not only in actual client/worker contact, but also in thinking and discussion with the supervisor, and perhaps also in college seminars and with the tutor.

However, one child in care was overheard by a student to say to another child, 'Don't get attached to your house-mother or social worker; they never stay and you won't see the same social worker again.'

The morality of using people for training in this way must be considered by the supervisor.

It is very difficult with most duty systems to ensure that a referral is completely new when it is handed to the student. Most clients have had some contact with the agency before the student takes on the case, and therefore may have pre-conceived expectations.

The supervisor and student need to work out together:

> Whether clients should be told that the worker is a student. Some agencies have set policies on this.

Whether clients should be told that the student is there
for a limited period only.

Clients frequently can accept that the worker is there only
on a part-time basis, but one has to be aware that as soon as
they know the date he is leaving, the relationship automatically moves into one of a time-limited contract, which may
not be the method of intervention advocated by the assessment of the situation. The timing of telling the client of the
termination or transfer is frequently critical (see chapter 8);
each case needs to be looked at individually by the supervisor
and student before a decision can be made.

Summary
Selection of cases is obviously restricted by the material
available, and the supervisor may not have the ideal cases to
give the student. Wherever possible, they should be selected
bearing in mind the student's previous knowledge and experience. It is desirable for the student to have experience of
most of the following areas of work:

children;
adolescents;
people who are inarticulate, aggressive, depressed/with-
drawn, dependent, manipulative, psychotic;
marital problems;
handicap — physical and mental;
problem families;
people of both sexes;
the elderly.

5 Recording

There have been allegations since all social work courses became generic, that social workers can no longer write reports. Confusion has arisen as to whether the teaching of report writing is the responsibility of the college or the field. Courses are under such pressure to include as much academic teaching as possible in an ever-widening field that frequently training in different methods of recording has been left to the field; supervisors with all their pressures, and perhaps themselves having received poor training in recording, often believe the responsibility to lie with the college. If both college and agency see themselves equally responsible, and the tutor and supervisor discuss the situation, these problems may be averted.

Purposes of Recording
As a teaching/learning tool (see Dwyer and Urbanowski 1965).
So that the supervisor knows what is going on in a particular case and can if necessary intervene to protect the client.
So that the agency has a record of the essential elements of work with a client/family. This is usually necessary for:
administrative purposes; if the worker is absent; or leaves the agency.
As a basis for consultation.

Methods of Recording
Experience indicates that there should be different kinds of recording to suit the different purposes outlined above, and that the students should be required from the beginning of their fieldwork training to prepare at least two kinds of records; one as a tool in the learning process, the other to meet agency requirements.

Process recording
Process recordings are useful tools in learning and teaching

social work. Initially, they may be difficult for the student to do, but they should become easier with practice. The record will always be a selective, subjective account of the student's recollection of what took place.

Framework of process recording. A good record should trace the interview chronologically from beginning to end and contain the following:

Date, place and length of time of the interview.

Physical circumstance of the interview; description of client's appearance; house, room if a home visit; the client's behaviour (gesture, posture, mannerisms, etc.). The significant conversational exchanges.

The student's feelings, thoughts and reactions to the client during the interview and his suggested reasons for these.

The student's assessment of the situation.

Summary, including what the student hoped to achieve together with what he did achieve.

Questions for supervision, e.g. factual information, assessment, how to handle the next interview, interpretations of content of interview. (See Butler and Elliott 1985 for a similar outline.)

The student may at first find that he is stilted in responses during the interview, in his effort to remember everything in order to record it, and also because of concern that he may be missing things and not making appropriate responses. It is useful if he can make comprehensive notes as soon as possible after the interview, whilst during the interview he tries to ignore the fact that he has to write a process recording on it. After he becomes more skilled in recording, these anxieties usually lessen. The student's thoughts after the interview should also be included.

Though other forms of recording for supervision are extremely valuable, the writing of a process record allows for a degree of reflection on the part of the student which is not obtainable by other methods, such as use of audio-tape recordings, video equipment and live supervision (see chapter 6). Process recordings need not be confined to work with individual clients, but can be extended to community or group work, to case conferences or work with other professionals.

Two examples are included in chapter 6 (Supervision). The first is a more traditional one and is self-explanatory; the second is written in three columns; one is blank, for the supervisor's comments; the centre one is for the process of the interview; the third is for the student's reflections, comments, observations and feelings. This model helps the student not to confuse his thoughts with the process of the interview. Some tutors and supervisors prefer to have some of the process recorded verbatim. In this case, the second model allows for a fuller picture of the content of the interview.

Process recordings are only seen by the supervisor, student and college tutor. They should be destroyed at the end of the placement. The recordings should be handed to the supervisor in good time before the supervision session, so that there is time to read and comment on them — it is useful if the supervisor makes comments in the margin. It is advisable for the student to make a carbon copy of the recordings if possible, so that he may be able to refer to them. College tutors should read the recordings before visiting the agency so as to be fully conversant with the practical work being done by the student.

The aims of process recording are not only to help to understand the client and his problem, but also to understand the interaction between client and student; thus the supervisor, student and college tutor become aware of how the student is working; what are the areas of strength and what are the ones needing more help. In this way, the student is also helped to find his best way of developing his own skills in order to help the client more effectively. It is useful if the student process records all first interviews and then selects one client, and process records all subsequent interviews. This not only demonstrates the development of the student, but traces the movement in the client.

Because they are to be seen by the college tutor, and are used as teaching material, it is advisable for purposes of confidentiality, if all process recordings are anonymous.

The process recording is a particularly valuable teaching tool for use with an inexperienced student who has yet to learn what is relevant in an interview and what is not. This is clearly demonstrated in the example given in the next chapter (chapter 6 — Supervision). This type of recording, together with the even more detailed verbatim recording (very difficult for the student to do with any degree of accuracy, except for occasional significant inter-changes), are the nearest the supervisor can get to knowing what exactly went on during the interview.

The supervisor is in a better position, having read a process recording, to teach the student what is significant and rela- tive. Questioning can elicit further information; for example, who changed the subject, student or client, and why?

Process recordings are very important, at least initially in the placement, as they help to bring to awareness areas which the student may be avoiding and the supervisor has not noticed.

Once the student has learnt to distinguish significant material in the interview, the importance of the process recording is not so great.

In the final placement, the supervisor and student may decide to do only occasional process recordings, or none at all, concentrating on teaching from other methods as by this stage, the student should know what is relevant in an interview and therefore be more able to be selective in the material brought to supervision; and should be spending less time in recording, and more in client contact than in earlier placements.

Agency recording

Examples of different frameworks for file records follow. It must be stressed that these examples are not meant to be comprehensive, or ideal in any way. In fact, many social workers think they can be greatly improved. They are no more than suggestions for ways of recording and have been collected from a number of different agencies.

Outlines included are:
  Social history
  Intake assessment
  Second and subsequent interviews
  Initial assessment summary
  Periodic summary
  Transfer summary
  Closing summary
  Juvenile court report.

Examples of the use of some of these for teaching material are given in the next chapter, on supervision.

Examples of Outlines for Recording

SOCIAL HISTORY

Name of Client	GP
Address	Address
Date of Birth	Tel.No.
Ethnic Origin	Religion

Reason for referral — i.e. presenting problem.

Informant — address, relationship to client (if not the client), description, any further relevant information.

Home conditions — including financial, number and state of rooms, etc.

Father — age, relationship with client and rest of family; any further relevant information.

Mother — ditto

Siblings — ditto

Personal history
Early childhood and development
School
Work

Sex — pre-marital
marriage
children — names, ages, any further relevant information

Health — physical and mental

Personality and interests

Summary and observations

INTAKE SYSTEM
FIRST INTERVIEW ASSESSMENT

1. *Referral*
   Who referred the client, and the reason for referral. Whether known to other agencies. Whether previously

known to this agency. Name, address, age, GP, details of family, other relevant factual information.

2. *Description*
   (a) *The client*, personal appearance, including any special characteristics, mannerisms, etc.
   (b) *The setting*. If appropriate: type of accommodation; how long in residence, etc. What this suggests about client.

3. *Affect*
   (a) the client's mood, e.g. happy, flat, etc.
   (b) his way of relating to the worker.

4. *How the problem is presented*
   (a) How it is stated — by the referee — by the client — how the two coincide.
   (b) What is seen to be most important, most urgent, by client.
   (c) What is implicit, but unstated.

5. *The interview*
   (a) Details of verbal and non-verbal interaction, including
   (b) Factual information
   (c) Feelings shown and expressed
   (d) Worker's participation
   (e) Movement during the first interview.

6. *Intervention plans*
   (a) Problems, areas agreed with client.
   (b) Time, place and frequency of interview (e.g. crises intervention, short- or long-term work).

7. *Summary*
   (a) Evaluative drawing together of client, problems, etc.
   (b) Attempt to assess total situations, including social and environmental influences and resources.
   (c) Formulative working method and techniques, e.g. (i) individual social work, family work, group or community work, or combinations; (ii) crisis intervention, task centred casework, long-term work, etc.

SECOND AND SUBSEQUENT INTERVIEWS

1. Brief comment on how the interview began and the emotional and physical state of the client.

2. Content of the interview.
   (a)   New factual information with the responses of both worker and client to these facts.
   (b)   A description of the way in which worker and client are relating or not relating to each other (i.e. what was happening at the feeling level).

3. Brief comment on the way in which the interview ended, with description of what has been agreed as the next step.

4. Summary: this would state how the client and his problems are seen now and would probably involve modification or elaboration of the summary made at the end of the first interview.

5. Questions for self and supervisor.

INITIAL ASSESSMENT SUMMARY

1. *Presenting problems*
   Referral source, reasons for referral, problems as stated in first interview if different from referral.

2. *Problems as they have emerged in subsequent interviews*
   This is to include other problems either recognised or unrecognised by the client or family. Details of earlier problems and information about the way in which present problems arose.

3. *The family*
   Description of each member of the family to include age, occupation, education, health and kind of person, if known.

   Description of the life style of the family (neighbourhood, housing, class, financial position, religion).

Description of the kind of relationships members of the family have with each other and how these seem to be affecting client or functioning of the family as a whole.

4. *The client*
   Physical description of the client, looks, physical health, manner of dress, special mannerisms or characteristics. Way of relating to worker, parents, authority, peers.

   Current functioning, i.e. how he is managing himself at home, at work and socially, indicating points of difficulty and reasons if known (e.g. low intelligence, difficulty in making relationships, anxiety, etc.). Characteristic modes of defence, if known.

5. *Psycho-social assessment*
   Description of the client's problem. This might include the type of problem in personal, physical and environmental terms.

   For example: This is an 80 year old man who is suffering from chronic bronchitis. Since his wife died five years ago he has been living alone in a rapidly deteriorating terrace house, in an area which is due for slum clearance. He is becoming increasingly confused, upsets the neighbours with his language and is not able to look after himself properly. He is reluctant to go into an old people's home.

6. *Intervention plans*
   This would be a description of the work already attempted with the client with comments about the client's response and ability to use a relationship with the worker for practical or/and personal help.

   Description of tentative plans for work with this client or family in the future.

7. *Questions*
   Questions and problems which the worker is struggling with.

Summaries
In addition to the interview summary and the initial diagnostic summary, students should be expected to write periodic

summaries, transfer summaries and closing summaries for the official file.

PERIODIC SUMMARY

This is a summary of the work done with a client/family over a period of time. Quarterly summaries seem to be realistic.

Outline
1. Dates covered (e.g. summary of work with X, 1.11.77– 31.1.78).

2. Number of interviews, where held and with whom, including comment on cancellations or not at home.

3. Description of the client and his problems at this point in time, highlighting environmental and personal changes during the period of work being summarised.

4. Summary of the work done during the period.

5. Comment on the quality of the relationship with the worker, indicating ups and downs and present position.

6. Comment on the extent to which original plans have been fulfilled or had to be modified.

7. Future plans.

TRANSFER SUMMARY

This is the summary which a worker should make when he has to leave the agency before a case is closed. It should indicate to the new worker, without him having to read the whole record, what this client's problems have been or are; the kind of work which has been done and the kind of help which the client and worker anticipate as being needed in the future.

Outline

1. Referral and presenting problems.

2. Problems as they have emerged during work with client/family.

3. Dates covered.

4. Number of interviews, pattern of interviews (weekly, monthly, etc.), where held and how arranged (e.g. letter, or popping in).

5. Description of the client and his problems at this point in time.

6. The kind of work attempted throughout the whole period of work with the client/family.

7. The quality of the relationship with the worker. Response to worker leaving.

8. Ways in which client sees himself as continuing to need help. Plans for new worker meeting client if arranged. (i.e. what the client knows about the new worker and what new worker will be told about the client.)

CLOSING SUMMARY

This is a summary which workers are so often reluctant to make, because they are unable to face the fact with their clients that the reason for which they came together in the first place has been resolved. It is important for students to learn in practice and demonstrate in recording that not every case needs to be kept going for ever and that cases can be re-opened.

Outline

1. Referral and presenting problems.

2. Problems as they have emerged during work with client/family.

3. Dates covered.

4. Number of interviews, pattern of interviews (weekly, monthly, etc.), where held and how arranged (e.g. letter, or popping in).

5. Description of the client and his problems at this point in time.

6. Comment on why both client and worker feel that the contact should end at this point. Plans for re-contacting agency if necessary might be commented on.

SUGGESTED PRO FORMA FOR COURT REPORTS

REPORT TO..............(name of Court and Date of Hearing)

Full name, date of birth   Religion
Address

Present case —   offence (brief), etc. of stealing, etc. and re-
                            manded to date

Previous court appearance(s):-
Date   Court   Offence (brief)   Result   (Do not include
                                                                        adjournments)

Particulars of family:

Father	Full names		Age	Occupation
Mother	"	"	"	"
S/Father	"	"	"	"
or Mother				
Children	"	"	d.o.b.	School (if known)
Subject to be underlined				
in d.o.b. order			"	"

Accommodation — Type of house — district — rooms —
                              rent/mortgage — condition

History of family
Birth — race — marriage particulars — stability — health — education — intelligence — evictions — rent arrears — employment — interests — known to social workers — help given. Children cared for — relationship with children — control over children — tolerance — friction — anxious.

Subject
Before school — starting school — health — serious illnesses, etc. — intelligence — demanding — difficult — delinquent — nature — attachment to parents — attitude to parents — sensitive — early riser — present school or employment — pastimes or hobbies — interest in sports and clubs — child guidance.

Present offence
Discuss with juvenile — outline of offence — juvenile attitude towards this — realisation of seriousness — remorse shown — future.

Observations
Summing up of case — recommendations, etc.

(Signed:).........................
Social Worker

Important in all written reports used for teaching purposes is, to have some idea of the interaction between student and client, and of the student's feelings and reactions. This is in order to ascertain whether a particular affect response in the student is one which the client frequently evokes in others, or whether it has sparked off some unresolved problem in the student.

Most agencies do not want detailed notes in the official file. People simply to not have the time to read pages of recording to elicit information. Therefore, students should from the beginning be asked to summarise the facts for the file, it having been made clear for what purpose these might be used at any time in the future in that particular agency.

Students need help in learning to write:
concise file records;
reports for other agencies and services, e.g. social histories, court reports — with a covering letter rather than report and letter mixed together;
they need to avoid long, confused reports which will never be read, or the giving of insufficient relevant information;
they should bear in mind for whom they are writing the reports. This may include the client (see below, Open files).

The supervisor should ensure that all file records are kept up-to-date, and should read the files regularly.

File records and agency summaries are another excellent teaching tool. The social worker will be helped by disciplined record keeping using definite frameworks, but this is frequently avoided for various reasons.

Initial summaries help to teach the student to assess and decide upon appropriate methods and techniques of intervention.

Periodic, transfer and closing summaries help in focusing on what has been achieved and what has not, and what is unrealistic.

It causes the worker to think what he and the client are doing and why, also indicating areas for future work.

Social histories: As well as learning how to record in this way, and how to gather information in a limited time, the student must be able to allow some time for the client to unburden himself and offer the client something, if only a sympathetic ear, so that he feels help is being given and he will want to return. Students find this sort of interviewing very difficult as it means introducing some structure, guidance, questioning and control into the interview.

A common difficulty students experience is learning again how to write concise file records after they have been trained in supervision to write process or verbatim reports. They have problems in selecting what is relevant for agency records and what is not, when they are being trained to see everything which takes place as relevant to some degree or other.

Open files: Client access to records
BASW (1983); DHSS (1983)

With the innovation of client access to records, many agencies have had to revise their standard ways of recording. Local authorities are drawing up their own policy documents and codes of practice, and devising new frameworks for recording. Already a variety of policies and frameworks exist (see Øvretveit 1985; Probert 1985). Discussions are still continuing as to the policy to apply in a number of areas, such as restricted material and the various ways in which this subject should be handled: whether client access should be retrospective or not; what should comprise the content of the file.

Consensus seems to be reached, in that fact and opinion should be clearly separated and that clients should know there are records kept and that they should be aware of the content. Suggested outlines for reports vary, but generally they do not appear to be incompatible with those included in this chapter.

Separate records may be kept for the social worker to use as 'working' models; this is similar to the process recordings used in student supervision. Recommendations are that these should be destroyed after a stated period. Though many people feel that a great deal of valuable material may be lost as a result of the policy, one of the implications is that social workers will have to think far more carefully when they are recording. Students are now being trained to record in line with the new policies.

6 Supervision

Methods of Teaching
These include:
Recording: process and agency records (see previous chapter) are useful learning tools. Examples of a process record and a social history are given later.
The weekly supervision session — see later.
The supervisor as a role model.
Continuous assessment (see chapter 7).
Various other methods, e.g. role play, use of audio-visual equipment; group discussions, formal and informal, in the agency; learning from other social workers in the agency.

The Supervision Session
In this chapter although the focus is on the individual supervision session, as most of the teaching and learning appears still to be concentrated there in the majority of agencies, comments on some other methods are included.

It is essential to have a regular weekly session of approximately 1½ hours. This must be seen by the student, supervisor and other social workers to take priority over all other demands on the supervisor's time. If importance is not given to this, the student may feel resentful, frustrated, angry; he is not being afforded his rights and it is difficult for a good teaching/learning relationship to develop and be sustained in this atmosphere. The student may feel that his needs are not being taken seriously, he is a nuisance, an imposition, or at best an extra cheap pair of hands in the agency.

Common difficulties for the supervisor, particularly a senior social worker in a busy social services department are:
Crises in the supervisor's own cases.
Crises in cases of other social workers accountable to him.
Important, urgent meetings (which abound in social services).
Telephone calls; some switchboard operators insist on putting calls through.

Finding a private room in which to supervise. If inter-viewing rooms are used, one may not always be available. The student and supervisor are then in the conflict situation of seeing supervision as taking second place to clients. If a room can always be made available, then the situation does not arise of having to decide whether clients or students take priority.

The student will need to know if or when the supervisor is available outside the set supervision time, for advice or consultation. He will also need to know who else to go to in the absence of the supervisor.

Both supervisor and student should prepare for the sessions: the student by giving in his written work in good time and by preparing a list of areas which he feels need discussing; the supervisor by having read and criticised the written work, noting the areas for discussion and teaching. Written comments on the process recordings are very helpful to student and supervisor and, later, to the college tutor who will then be informed of the points already discussed.

It is very disheartening for the student if the supervisor makes no comments, written or verbal, on his process record-ings. It is even worse, of course, if they are not always read by the supervisor. This has been known to occur; it dimin-ishes the value of the reports and the student is justifiably very angry as he has put into them so much effort.

The actual teaching in the session may consist of:

Factual information about agency limits, policy, re-sources, etc.

Relation of theory to practice. This includes a know-ledge of the social and behavioural sciences, theories of personality, psychopathology, social work method and theory. Application of these is the central part of teach-ing in the placement. Students may need guidance in how to listen, question, observe; how and when to intervene (see Cross 1974; Garrett 1972; Kadushin 1976; Keith-Lucas 1972; Butler and Eliott 1985). It is important for supervisors to be able to generalise from specific case material and to help the student explore underlying meanings of clients' behaviour.

The student needs to have spelt out to him his areas of strength and weakness; praise and constructive criticism are necessary throughout, and make up part of the continuous assessment (see chapter 7). The student then knows exactly where he is, and is freer to discuss his progress more openly with his supervisor.

Though teaching from recordings is important, it is equally important for the supervisor and student to be flexible, discovering together their particular best combination of methods for the teaching/learning process (see later).

Some Problems in Learning

The supervisor and student need to develop a relationship of trust whereby free interchange of ideas may take place, so that learning is facilitated. Within this relationship, problems such as the boundary between teaching and casework may not become insuperable, but may be seen in the context of developing student self-awareness and of removing resistances to learning and blocks to effective work with clients; e.g. he may be defending himself against examination of his feelings towards his clients.

If problems between supervisor and student do develop, each should feel free to suggest asking the college tutor into the agency to help sort things out.

The tutor may be needed to help if the supervisor detects in the student a problem in working which he has, still unresolved, in himself. Open acknowledgement is necessary in order to sustain the relationship of respect and trust.

Anxiety levels in the student have to be handled with care and expertise by the supervisor; the student may need help in containing anxiety about a client until the supervision session; he may need help in withstanding the client's efforts to give him (the student) all his (the client's) anxiety, depression, etc., and leave freed, having handed his burden to the worker. The supervisor has to assess the level of anxiety in the student and decide what is appropriate for learning purposes, and what is inappropriate, and operating against maximum development.

Transference and countertransference feelings can cause great difficulties, particularly if they pass unrecognised. These have been discussed elsewhere (chapter 3). Overinvolvement or over-detachment which are associated problems, also operate against student learning.

The expected period of depression mid-way through the course (see chapter 3) need not be an impediment, but can on the contrary, prove to be a valuable experience in the student's professional development.

Other difficulties may include dependency/independency problems; problems associated with authority; the student not being fully occupied; undisciplined teaching approach.

The supervisor should always remember that he is a role-model.

Examples of Process Recordings

PROCESS RECORDING

4.6.80   10.30 a.m. − 11.30 a.m.   Address:
First visit to Miss J., aged 20 years.

Reason for referral
Client referred herself by coming to the office two days ago, with a letter from landlord saying she would be evicted in a month's time; wants help with accommodation, as is in furnished bed-sitter. She was told that someone would visit.

Miss J. lives in a bed-sitter in a small cul-de-sac, where all the two-storey, terraced houses have a peeled, dilapidated look, with faded, grimy paint on the few gates that are left, one or two bald hedges straggling the divisions between the front yards (I do not feel that I could possibly call them gardens, as there is no grass to be seen, and I feel sure they have never seen a flower in their lives). As I walked along, looking for No. 6, several women, arms akimbo, hair in curlers and bedroom slippers on their feet, stopped gossiping in the doorways as I passed, to stare at me until I had moved on to the next house. There was a pervading air of hostility around, and I felt that I was not in anonymous bedsitter land, but in a close-knit subculture, where any stranger was unwelcome, and looked on with suspicion.

I went into No. 6 and knocked. After a moment or two, the door opened a crack, and a grey haired, elderly, unkempt woman peeped out. I asked if Miss J. were in, and she nodded, opening the door a little more, to reveal that she had been trying to restrain a dog from rushing out. She pointed up the stairs, calling out to Miss J. that there was 'The Welfare to see you'. (I had not introduced myself!) Miss J. came into sight at the top of the dark, bare, uncarpeted stairs (brown and green paint everywhere, narrow corridors and no light) and smilingly asked me to come up, explaining apologetically that she had not heard me ring. She showed me into her room, which faced the back of the house, overlooking the small garden, where the faded grass struggled with the few dusty flowers, to look cheerful under the glare of the weak, summer sun peeping through the one tired tree. Her room was certainly small, but she had tried to make it cheerful, and it was clean. Two old, comfortable armchairs, a bed, cot and table were about all the furniture she had, but she had put colourful posters on the walls, and had cheerful scatter cushions around. There was a double gas ring in the corner, and a wash basin. The baby was asleep in the cot.

Miss J. looked a very young 20, with long, mousy hair, no make-up, and wearing a powder blue jumper (classic style) and black wool skirt. She had a pale complexion, a round face, and enormous, innocent looking grey eyes; she was short, and very thin.

I started the interview, after she had motioned me to sit in one of the armchairs (the one with the back to the window, she took, and I was facing) by saying that I understood she was to be evicted. She replied, in an uninterested way, 'Oh yes, we all are.' I asked who 'all' were, and she said that the rest of the house was let to her brother, sister-in-law and their four children, and that it was to be modernised and then re-let. She was then silent, so I asked her who was the woman who let me in, and she replied that it was probably her sister-in-law's mother; she lived next door, and always had; it was through her that the others had got the house to rent, and they had persuaded the landlord to let her have a room when she had the baby. She then jumped up and rushed to the cot, saying 'Don't you think he's beautiful?' I was a bit annoyed at her changing the subject — perhaps she was denying the predicament she was in, with a baby and impending eviction. I said yes, without getting up to look, and asked her if she had tried to find anywhere else to live. She appeared surprised, and slowly went back to her chair, saying that she really hadn't had time to think about it. Her brother was hoping to get a large flat, but there would not be room for her, and anyway, he had not spoken to her since she became pregnant. I was surprised at this seeing she lived in the same house, and queried it, but she said that her sister-in-law had arranged it all, and she spoke to her, but only when her brother was out. I asked her how soon she would have to move, but she did not reply directly; she got up, moved to the window, and looking out, said that she had been made quite welcome here, which was strange, as she had not been brought up in the street, she had been here ever since she left the mother and baby home. She then went over and shook the cot, but the baby still slept; she cooed and talked to it, and I became increasingly irritated because she would not keep to the point of the conversation, and did not seem to be taking her position seriously. I tried again, feeling exasperated. I asked her when her brother would be moving out; again she looked surprised, picked the baby up (unnecessarily, I thought, as it meant waking it up and causing further interruption to the subject). She said she had not asked her sister-in-law, and in any event they could not evict her yet, as the landlord had not even instigated court proceedings. This showed me that she did indeed know something of the situation she was in and was obviously in no hurry to do anything about it. Miss J. brought the baby close to me so that I could see him, and again asked me if I didn't think he was beautiful. I said yes, I did, and asked her how she managed for money; she said she lived on social security and could just about cope, but she would probably find it more difficult as the baby got older — he was now nearly 3 months, and she did not have any maintenance. I asked if she applied to the court for any, but she said that she had not heard of the father since she told him she was pregnant — the baby looked very like his father, and was a constant reminder. I wondered aloud, if she knew where he was, and could perhaps try to take him to court at this stage, but she said no, it was all too painful and she didn't want to think about it. I hardly felt she was prepared to help herself, and was somewhat puzzled at her lack of motivation, but forbore to say so.

There was a short silence, while I wondered how to get back to the subject of accommodation, when she suddenly said that she had not told her parents about the baby, and was not sure whether or not her brother had. I asked if they wouldn't provide a home for her if she were really stuck, and she looked at me in horror, saying they would never speak to her again if they knew what had happened, as they were very strict Catholics; she had not been to Mass since she knew she was pregnant.

Miss J. was giving all her attention to the baby now, and pretty well ignoring me; I felt at a loss, as every time I tried to talk about her problems, she talked about the baby, or her brother or family. Consequently, I thought I would retreat to safe subjects, to try and establish a better relationship, and get her to lower her defences a bit and trust me. I asked if she had many friends around, or managed to go out much. She replied, shrinking into herself as she held the baby protectively, and looking wary and scared, that she didn't talk to people much, as they always seemed to let you down when you began to get involved with them; I presumed she was talking about men, so I asked her about girl friends, and she said that she used to have a lot at home in Ireland, in her small, country village, but that she had not met many over here, in spite of having worked in a factory for some time.

After some more irrelevant talk along these lines, I tried to make some other comment — I forget exactly what — about the impending eviction, but felt completely non-plussed when she did not seem to hear me, but looked tearfully at the baby, saying that she wished he did not look so like his father! I was not sure whether or not to offer her another visit, so I asked if she wanted me to call again. She said, 'Yes, if you want to'. I was not sure how to take this, but made another appointment for the same time next week. She saw me to the top of the stairs, still holding the baby, but did not smile as I went down.

Summary and observations

I was not at all sure what to make of this client or her problem. She obviously had been worried enough about the eviction to make the effort to come to the office, but seemed completely determined not to talk about it when I was there — in fact she seized everything she could to turn the subject away from that. Was she very defensive, denying there was a problem? How is she really coping with money, and why does she not seem bothered to get maintenance? I wonder if she panicked into coming to the office when she had the notice to quit, but now is pretending it will never happen. I also cannot understand how she seemed so pleased to see me when I arrived, but I lost her pretty quickly, and could not get any rapport again, however hard I tried.

Goals:
Short term: to make her look at her problem and try to motivate her to do something about it herself; weekly visiting at present, in the hopes this goal may be realised before she is evicted. To prevent reception into homeless accommodation.
Long term: to help her to adjust more effectively to her situation, possibly getting a job and having the child minded.
For supervisor: As well as the above questions, I would like to comment that I am not at all sure really what is going on here, or whether there is any real need for us to continue to be involved, unless it is to prevent homelessness.

This example demonstrates clearly a number of things.
It is an excellent process recording in that it gives a clear picture of the area the client lived in, the client herself, her attitudes, the interaction with the student, the feelings of both client and student. It reveals the stage the student is at and gives the supervisor a very clear idea of the areas in which the student needs immediate help. It fulfils most of the demands of a process recording (see chapter 5).
Some of the points immediately arising in supervision from this would be:
Did the supervisor brief the student adequately before the visit (see chapter 2)? The student obviously went in feeling he had to obtain information on the practical issue of housing, and give help in this area; consequently he was unable to listen to what the client really was saying, and became increasingly preoccupied with his own anxiety surrounding his belief that he had to return to his supervisor without either having collected any relevant information or of having been able to offer practical assistance. The supervisor's evaluation of his performance was probably also causing him anxiety, and his frustration and irritation were reacted to by the client.
The student needed teaching on the subject of presenting problems, and how to distinguish between these and underlying problems.
He needed a great deal of help in learning how to listen;

he obviously was ignorant of the whole subject of non-verbal interaction, though his powers of observation were good.

He did not understand the importance of discovering where the client is, staying with the client, and of understanding the problems as seen by her.

Ideas of making a contract with the client did not appear to have entered into his thinking. He was trying to impose his own perception of a previous, preliminary assessment, on to the client.

He had not begun yet to develop skills of making preliminary assessments and being able later to modify them in the light of new information; he tried to fit the client into a preconceived picture and became distressed when she did not co-operate.

He had not included the client in any discussion or decision making surrounding their working together on certain problem areas, with specific foci in mind. Because of the frustration on both sides, his own and the client's, he may well have lost the client.

The supervisor must realise the importance of giving praise and encouragement to the student, as well as being critical of his work in a facilitating way. In this instance, the actual recording is worthy of praise, as is the way in which the student is able to draw vivid word pictures and reveal his own inmost feelings throughout. He was able to provide his supervisor with useful teaching material. His potential for movement was revealed by his awareness that he had not understood at all what was going on.

STUDENT'S COMMENTS	VERBATIM/P.R.	SUPER-VISOR'S COMMENTS
Felt that she was pleased to see me and felt more relaxed than initial visit.	Mrs S opened the door in a welcoming fashion with a nice smile. This week she looked more relaxed and younger, dressed smartly in trousers and top. She immediately sat next to me on the sofa and I took my coat off.	

STUDENT'S COMMENTS	VERBATIM/P.R.	SUPERVISOR'S COMMENTS
	'So, how have you been this last week?' 'Well, to tell you the truth I have been quite bad. Everything seems to have gone wrong. There has been a confusing letter from the civil service, I never know exactly what they're asking for. Still I haven't got my pension book, so I just phoned up social security and they said that they would send it off tonight. I did enquire like you said about the bars for the window — but they're going to cost £50 which I can't afford, so I bought a lock for the window which I put up this morning.'	I think you handled the beginning of the interview very well, especially following on from last week when you didn't know why you were going.
	'I'm impressed — I don't think I'd tackle a job like this — I suppose that's a problem now, learning to do things which formerly your husband would have done.'	Lovely. I like the way you gave her credit and confidence to share good things about herself.
	'Well, that's right — I've even learnt to do a plug, which I'm pleased about' (smile). 'Actually my friend phoned up and she says she might have some bars that will fit, so her fitter is coming round tonight to check it all out.'	
	'Presumably you feel a bit safer here now?'	

STUDENT'S COMMENTS	VERBATIM/P.R.	SUPER-VISOR'S COMMENTS
	'Well, not really, because the lock was only put on this morning. Though because I was so tired last week I slept well. And I've been thinking, that although my neighbour is nice and everything, she makes me nervous by always talking about burglaries. I wish in a way she wouldn't tell me — because I wasn't at all nervous when I first came back to the house.'	
	'Did you go to the District Housing Office?'	
Was pleased she'd done this herself and that I hadn't taken on the job myself as she'd originally requested.	'Yes, but there's nothing much there, the only place I was interested in to move to, the people there wanted to move to the country, so that was no good. And actually, I've been thinking that I'll stay here after all. For one thing, I couldn't afford new carpets and curtains, and what I've got might not fit, you know. Also this place isn't so bad. I know it's an estate, but it's not really like one, no vandals or graffiti; and things.'	Would it have been possible to remind her that last week this aspect she had asked you to do and she has actually done it herself effectively? Reaffirm that she's doing some things very well.
	'I'm pleased you've decided to stay. A move just now would be a lot to think about, what with everything else. Tell me, have you been out at all, or has anybody called?'	

STUDENT'S COMMENTS	VERBATIM/P.R.	SUPER-VISOR'S COMMENTS
	'Not really. It's funny when my husband was alive, the house was always full of people — in fact, like on a Sunday, I used to wish we could be by ourselves. But now nobody. It's weird.'	
Felt that the transition from housing practicalities to coping with bereavement went smoothly. I didn't feel I was being nosey. Had hoped to get round to feelings of death naturally and sensitively. Don't feel I 'bulldozed'.	'You know, after a death this sort of thing often happens. There are lots of callers immediately after the death, then people stop calling. I think that people are often embarrassed. They don't know what to say.' 'That's right, because one friend called and said she would have before, but didn't know what to say. But I didn't know . . .'	Yes, I agree — a smooth way in to talking about something which is quite difficult for you. You have felt like this too, haven't you? We must discuss it more.

This is only the first part of the interview. The student previously expressed anxiety and resistance to the idea of bereavement counselling. This piece of recording shows how she was able to start doing it, with her own feelings recorded separately, together with the critically supportive comments of the supervisor.

The example of this style of process recording was referred to in the previous chapter. By recording in columns, the supervisor's comments are easy to see, and the student is helped to keep separate fact and opinion. This is an essential thing to learn from the beginning of training in the light of client access to records.

An Example of a Social History

SOCIAL HISTORY

Name of client: Miss S.   *GP:* Dr B.
Address: *Address*
Date of birth: 24.6.59. Aged 26 years   *Telephone No:*

Referred by self for R.I.C. of 5 year old daughter.

Informant: Client

Home conditions:
Miss S. lives in a newly built one bedroomed council flat, which she has occupied since it was completed one year ago. Prior to that she was in homeless accommodation for 3 months since eviction from furnished accommodation. The flat is in a tower block, with Miss S. on the first floor; it is sparsely, but adequately furnished, not very clean, with only a doll and a few books around for the child, Susan. There are a few tins in the kitchen, by way of food. A rented television and stereo record player are noticeable in the living room. Miss S. lives on social security except for the occasional weeks when she has a factory job (child left with anyone who will look after her, who knows her).

Family history:
Father: Unknown.
Mother: Died when client 12 years. Little known, except that she placed client in care when client was a baby (6 months); used to visit about once a year until Miss S. 4 years old, then ceased. Occasional letters after. Married when client 3 years old.
Step-siblings: About 4, all younger than client, and children of the marriage. Never been any contact, and whereabouts unknown by Miss S.

Personal history:
Early childhood and development: Illegitimate, and placed in residential nursery at 6 months, as mother could not afford to keep her; mother visited occasionally until

marriage and other children.

Normal milestones, as far as is known.

Transferred to children's home after two abortive attempts at fostering (client thinks mother complained — jealous of à relationship developing with foster mother, as always said she would soon take her out of care; Miss S. told this by housemother) aged 5 years.

School: Below average. Was never interested. Many transient friendships. Not very happy memories. Left as soon as she could. Never thought of whether she liked children's home or not; opted out of any trouble; quiet, somewhat withdrawn.

Work: Numerous assembly line factory jobs, average duration 3—6 months. Loses interest very quickly.

Sex: Many superficial relationships with boys. No current boyfriend.

Children: Miscarriage when she was 18.
Susan aged 5 years.
Abortion 2 years ago.

Susan: Enuretic, shy, insecure, withdrawn, pale, thin child. Has been at school for one term, and showing signs of school refusal. Tearful and clinging to mother during interview. Mother says she cannot cope with her demands, now that she is getting older, and complains of constant crying and temper tantrums; petty pilfering has started from mother and at school. Always been feeding difficulties. R.I.C. aged 1, for 6 weeks; aged 2 for 10 weeks.

Health: Physical: good.
Mental: 2 hospital admissions for depression, due to inability to cope, 4 years and 3 years ago, coinciding with child being in care. Infrequent attendance at out-patients since.

Personality and interests:
Can cope as long as no great demands are made, and while she can be dependent on others. Wants to be entertained all the time, and resents having to stay in to look after child. Likes dancing, cinema, etc. No close friends, sees having a good time as her right and dislikes idea of responsibility. Annoyed if child shows any sign of independence, or crosses her in any way, but feels she ought to keep her with her. Now becoming increasingly anxious and depressed again with demands made on her.

Summary and observations: Inadequate, emotionally deprived girl, who is very limited in what she is able to give her child. Reacts with anxiety and depression when demands on her are too great.
Goal: long-term support; uncritical acceptance and encouragement in order to help her learn to relate, feel cared for, provide a more stable environment for child, and keep out of financial trouble.

Writing social histories helps the student to learn to elicit information by guiding, unobtrusively, a basically unstructured interview. Students frequently have difficulty in bringing themselves to ask clients direct questions, for fear of intruding into areas of privacy, even when clients expect this. This problem can best be dealt with in the supervision setting, each time it occurs in a specific case, as appropriate reasons can then be given to the student for the need for the apparent intrusion.

Associated with this are the anxieties the student experiences about whether or not to write down anything factual during the interview, and if so, how to broach this with the client.

Writing a social history after an interview highlights areas where there may be gaps, so that the student and supervisor may look at possible reasons for this. Has the student a problem of resistance in this area? Is the resistance in the client? Is the area irrelevant? In the final case, relevance can only be decided on the basis of complete information.

This is a good means for teaching assessment skills. The student and supervisor can then work out the probable prognosis and the method of social work intervention most likely to afford the best results.

Example of an Intake Interview

INTAKE INTERVIEW IN A GENERAL
SOCIAL WORK AGENCY

Date of   X *FAMILY*
contract February 198—

19 February 198—. Report of Duty Interview with: Mrs X.

Referral:

Mrs X. came into the office asking for advice and support
re 'family troubles'. She said she had been prompted to
come after a family quarrel on Sat. night/Sun. morning
during which her husband hit the eldest son, 17 yrs, and
she had called the police. They had not taken any action
but advised her to seek the help of a social worker.

The X. family were previously known to Miss I., School
Health Service (about 3 yrs. ago). In the past she has also
had some contact with the F.W.A. At present Mrs X. is not
in touch with any social work agency.

Descriptive:

Mrs X. is a large over-weight lady aged 45 yrs. She was
dressed in a glamorous-looking fur coat but had a torn
overall on underneath, a summer frock and no make-up;
she looked very tired and worried.

Mrs X. appeared at first to be of limited intelligence but
this may have been a result of her depression and anxiety
state. In addition Mrs X. is almost completely deaf and
suffers from a speech defect; she lip-reads very well.

Family:

Married (Husband:	50 yrs.	Electrician	
20 yrs. (Wife:	45 yrs.	Shop Assistant	
Children:G	18 yrs.	Petrol Pump Attendant	
B	17 yrs.	employment N/K to Social Worker	
B	11 yrs.	School	
B	6 yrs.	"	

Affect:

Mrs X. said she felt very depressed and in fact spent much of the time crying and then apologising for this. She did not seem to be very relaxed and fiddled constantly with the edge of her overall in an anxious manner.

I felt that she had some difficulty relating to me as a social worker and on several occasions said that 'no-one really understood her problems' and that 'they' kept passing her 'case' around and no-one was 'doing anything'. She added that she had got on extremely well with Miss I. who had visited her over a long period but since then had not met a social worker who had been able to 'help her'.

During the first part of the interview Mrs X. tended to look down thus I had some difficulty talking to her and had to wait until she had completely finished before I could come in.

In spite of this however Mrs X. responded reasonably well to most of my questions and was able to express herself freely.

Problems:

Mrs X. saw the main problem as being the need to 'get something done' about the family and marital problems and so prevent the two younger boys suffering in the same way as the two elder children had. She said that her husband 'got on quite well' with the children when they were young but once they reached their middle teens he 'picked on them' due, she said, to his jealousy of them.

She was ambivalent however about her future plans and said she wanted some legal advice re the possibility of a separation and also support in coming to terms with the situation.

I felt that Mrs X. not only wanted someone to talk to but also wanted me to make any decisions for her.

Interview:

The interview took place in the Area Office interviewing room and lasted about 45 mins.

Mrs X. began by telling me that she was deaf but could lip-read if I spoke slowly. She then went on to say that she had seen several social workers in the past and I would be able to understand her problems better if I read the file first and had some idea of the history of the case.

She spent most of the first part of the interview talking about the events of the last few days and made several vague allusions to incidents in the past. She appeared to have a great need to talk about these things and eventually broke down in tears and cried freely for about 10 mins. After this Mrs X. was more relaxed and coherent and responded much better to my questions and showed some insight into the situation.

Mrs X. said that there had been marital problems for as long as she could remember and in fact she and her husband had led separate lives for the past 6 yrs in that they had separate bedrooms, ate separately and very rarely spoke to each other. On several occasions he had said he was going to leave them but had never gone. They have been married 20 yrs.

At this point Mrs X. talked about her own family background and said that her parents had separated when she was about 6 yrs old and she had grown up with her mother. She saw her background as being a middle-class one while her husband was working class; she felt that this had contributed to the breakdown in their relationship.

As well as the marital problem we discussed Mr X's relationship with the two eldest children. It seems that he tends to pick on them for little or no reason and accuses them of staying out late, drinking, taking drugs etc. and this invariably provokes a quarrel. Mrs X. said that she feared the same thing would happen when the two youngest, now 11 and 6 yrs, grew up and she wanted to do something now to prevent this situation recurring. In her opinion the 'cause' of the problem was her husband's jealousy of her close relationship with the children. She said she was sometimes over-protective in that she protected them from him. As examples she quoted S's court appearance for non-attendance at school about 5 yrs ago and the time when L gave up his job and was unemployed for a few weeks; she had kept both of these incidents from her husband although she had felt guilty about it.

Mrs X. also talked a lot about her own feelings. Although she said her husband was difficult to live with, she appeared to accept some of the 'blame' for the problems herself and said she knew she 'was not an angel'. She said she suffered from frequent fits of depression, cried a lot and sometimes went off for long walks on her own. Her husband had often said she was 'mental', but when she tried to seek the help of a psychiatrist, her GP had rejected the idea.

Mrs X. also said that her husband was not usually violent, did not drink heavily and there were no debts other than HP for furniture.

Problems as agreed with client:
1. Relationship problems with family.
2. Mrs X's need for emotional support.

Action:
1. As Mrs X. said she was planning to see her GP tonight, I encouraged her in this. She appears to have a good relationship with him.
2. In view of the legal aspects of separation and tenancy of the flat, I suggested Mrs X. go to either L.A.C. or the Probation Officer at Court. I gave her these addresses.
3. I also gave her my name, address and telephone number and suggested she contact me when necessary.

We discussed the possibility of her going back to F.W.A., but she rejected this saying that she had not found them helpful in the past.

Summary:
Mrs X. expressed a great many emotions during the interview, but seemed much more relaxed by the time she left. In the past couple of years, Mrs X. has coped with the various problems herself but has tended to live from 'crisis to crisis'. She has some awareness of the problems and some insight, thus I think she would respond to and benefit from some casework help. However, she is not sure if her husband would agree to see a social worker.

Records of Practical Work
It is very useful if the supervisor and student keep an up-to-date record of the practical work done. This might include:
List of clients/families, with
Dates of interviews (and therefore frequency).
Whether each is a home visit or office interview, with reasons.

Whether the file record has been done on each.
Whether a process recording has been made.
Whether a social history, social inquiry report or similar report has been made.
The assessment and intervention plans.
Other activities engaged in by the student. These might include:
Visits to other agencies.
Participation in groups.
Meetings.
Record-keeping of this sort can highlight problems the student may have in areas such as disciplined recording; making appointments with clients; regular, planned interviews; overall plan of work with set goals.

Supervisory Notes
It is helpful for both the supervisor and the student to keep notes on the supervisory sessions. With the charted record of practical work outlined in the previous section, and the supervisory notes, the evaluation is virtually written as the placement progresses.

Other Methods of Practical Work Teaching
Experiments and developments in other methods of practical teaching are constantly taking place; these do not usually replace individual supervision, but are used as an additional different learning experience.
A few examples follow.

Team supervision
In this model of practical work teaching, the whole social work team is responsible for supervising the student or students. However, it is usually found to be impractical unless one team member is given overall responsibility. This avoids confusion for the student, clarifies problems of accountability, and enables the college tutor to have a specific person to contact. The named social worker would also be responsible for administrative details relating to the student and college, e.g. for seeing that the evaluation was written.
The principal advantages of team supervision are:
the accessibility to the student of a wide range of experience and expertise;

SOCIAL WORK RECORD CHART

Client/s	Problem	Theories & Methods Used	Time Span; Number & frequency of interviews	Work done	Outcome

Example of Outline for Practical Work Record

a sharing of the responsibility of teaching amongst a number of workers.

The disadvantages include the facts that:

some student problems may go undiscovered;

the student may feel unable to approach anyone specifically if he is aware of a problem.

In a flexible agency the advantages of team supervision can be used in conjunction with the traditional supervision model; there is no reason why the student and supervisor need not approach all team members when necessary, using them in the fieldwork teaching. In fact this usually does occur in agencies where students are accepted as an integral part of the team.

A particular example of this is in the various combinations of individual or conjoint marital and/or family work where it is increasingly common for a number of social workers to be supervising students and other workers. As clients are seen less as individuals in isolation, and more as members of their families and wider environments, these models of teaching are likely to be used far more extensively, though not exclusively, they throw up problems which need very skilful and expert handling and may therefore be unsuitable models for the new supervisor. More detailed discussion is outside the scope of this book and interested readers are advised to consult marital and family therapy literature.

Where they exist and where it is appropriate, group and community workers may also be involved in team supervision.

Group supervision (see Kaslow 1977)

This is a useful model of practical teaching which is different from individual supervision and as such does not necessarily replace it.

One fieldwork teacher supervises a group of students together. This may be the same person as the individual supervisor or the worker who has overall responsibility for the student unit.

A variety of teaching methods may be used, for example:

Students may present in turn cases for discussion using different recording frameworks.

Students may present cases verbally.

Students may present specific topics for discussion.

The supervisor may present specific topics for discussion.

Other social workers or people in related professions may be invited to conduct seminars on specific topics.

Role play may be used as a learning aid.

Students may be involved in an experiential group.

Advantages of group supervision:

This model of teaching is of immeasurable value to students who are on courses where the material is presented mainly in lecture form as opposed to seminar form. It enables them to have the opportunity to explore their own ideas, sharing them and their experiences with those of their fellow students and workers.

Disadvantages of group supervision:

Where the students are all at different stages in training, coming from a variety of colleges, it is very difficult to find common teaching subjects and treat them at a level which will be useful to all of the students.

A result of this is that topics may be dealt with on a superficial level, leaving some students feeling frustrated.

Where this method of teaching is used extensively by the college, as it is on many courses, the students may find it repetitive and feel valuable time is being misused on a short and pressurised course.

Audio-tape recording and audio-visual materials are being used increasingly often and are valuable aids to learning, as are the use of a one-way screen (see Star 1979).

In situations such as marital and family therapy (see Kaslow 1977) it is now common to have either live supervision, whereby the supervisor is a co-worker and the interview is discussed fully afterwards, or open supervision during the interview (see Butler and Elliott 1985). These are direct methods of supervision, in contrast to the indirect ones described above.

Students who are placed in situations other than fieldwork need methods of teaching appropriate to their specific agency. These are comprehensively described elsewhere, e.g.

Groupwork supervision (see Martel 1981; Kaslow 1977)

Community work supervision (see Briscoe and Thomas 1977)

Residential and day care (see Payne and Scott 1982).

Summary
These methods of practical teaching are important and valuable, but it is probably short-sighted to apply them indiscriminately and without discretion, just as it is to assume that they alone are adequate in supplying practical training which social workers nowadays require.

Ideally, the supervisor should work out with the student and tutor the appropriate teaching methods, taking into account the individual needs of the student but not losing sight of the aims of training. This will help the student to make maximum use of the placement as a learning experience.

In discussing models of teaching, it should never be forgotten that the object of the placement is for the student to learn to be a practical social worker. There is an ever present danger of a disproportionate amount of time being spent in discussion groups, at the expense of client contact.

Additional Information
An example of guidelines which may be sent out from the college to the supervisor to help him in teaching the student follows. Most of the points in it have been discussed elsewhere.

GUIDELINES FROM COLLEGE TO SUPERVISOR

1. Please give students limited caseload:
   3—4 on-going cases in first placement.
   Up to 6—8 on-going cases in final placement.

2. Process recordings:
   Essential in first placement.
   Preferably one on each initial interview; *and* continuous ones on same client/family.
   (a) to show development of student's skills;
   (b) relationship developed;
   (c) work done;
   (d) highlights difficult areas;
   (e) shows interviewing techniques;
   (f) shows how student handles situations, etc.

3. Social history. Inquiry, etc., on at least one case.

4. It is helpful if supervisors make written comments on the process recordings. Students can then refer back to these. Common teaching areas include:
    Feeding the client: putting the answer the student expects into the question.
    How the student handles silences.
    Student's own reaction to client and what he says.
    Subject change: who changed it, student or client, and why.
    Student's observations — backed by evidence from the interview.

5. Students need help in seeing the pattern in any situation:
    The developmental picture which influences present behaviour.
    The environmental/social influences.
    The intellectual capacity.

6. This helps to train students in assessing. They can then plan their goals in more realistic terms, and are integrating their theoretical learning with their practical work.

7. Students are helped to organise their information and see frameworks if, at the end of each process recording and any interview whether process recorded or not, they list:
    their observations and conclusions, with evidence;
    their assessment of the present situation;
    their short-term and long-term goals;
    whether they have or not achieved the aims they set in this particular interview.

8. The supervisor helps by adding to this, helping the student to focus realistically.

9. Direct observation and monitoring:
    Supervisors are encouraged to take the opportunity to observe directly the student at work. This can take the form of any of the following:

participant observation; live supervision; watching the student's performance in a formal or public setting, e.g. in court or at a case conference; listening to tape recordings of student's work; observing video tapes of student's work.

10. Compiling the report:

Towards the end of the placement and before the submission of the fieldwork teacher's report, a discussion will take place between the supervisor, the student and the tutor. The ideal state of affairs here is that nothing that is discussed at this meeting, and nothing that appears in the fieldwork teacher's assessment of the student should come as a surprise to the student. Assessment is a continuous process during the placement and that the practice teacher should share views about the student's performance with him or her as and when the issues arise.

The final evaluation report should contain a clear recommendation at the end, as to whether, in the supervisor's opinion, the student has satisfactorily completed the placement and met the criteria outlined or whether he is deemed to have failed. In cases of an exceptionally high standard of performance a recommendation may be made to the examining board that students be awarded a pass with distinction.

It is usual for the evaluation report to contain the signatures of both the practice teacher and student, but in exceptional cases of irresolvable disagreement, the student may write an addendum to the report.

7 Evaluation and Aims of the Placement

This chapter deals primarily with fieldwork placements, but this does not deny the value of other placements.

Other placements include those in residential, community work, or social groupwork settings. These types of placement, together with those in allied services, e.g. housing, are important, particularly as the emphasis in teaching has changed from an exclusively focused one-to-one casework approach to a family and unitary approach.

Most courses include some placements apart from those in fieldwork. The value of gaining experience in a range of agencies cannot be denied, but it is impossible for a student on a generic course to have a placement in every type of setting and therefore selection must take place.

Some common aims of these alternative or additional placements, for example, in a residential placement, are:

To gain experience of working in a residential setting.

To become aware of the sort of difficulties likely to be experienced by residential social workers.

To develop an understanding of the attitudes and frustrations of these workers and to understand their relationships with other social workers, professionals and agencies.

To gain an insight into the feelings of the residents.

To observe the process of institutionalisation.

Aims of Fieldwork Placements

Below are examples of information given by a college to the fieldwork supervisors, outlining the aims of a first placement and those of the final placement. Though these are only examples, and courses may vary in their expectations and requirements, most colleges have similar aims.

The supervisor needs to have some guidelines such as those set out, particularly if he has only one student from the course, otherwise he has no base against which to measure his student's performance and development. Contacts with the tutor and supervisors' meetings (see chapter 2) are the other means whereby he can judge where his student is in relation to the rest of the student group.

As well as needing to know where a student is at the beginning of the placement, the supervisor needs to know where the college expects him to be at the end, so he has a definite set of goals towards which he and the student are working.

If the supervisor is not given such guidelines by the tutor, it is in order for him to ask for them.

GUIDE FOR CRITERIA FOR ASSESSMENT OF FIELDWORK

First Placement

1. *Caseload*
   This should be very limited, building up to between 4 to 6 cases as student needs
   (a) to develop relationships and develop ability to use these over a period of time;
   (b) to have time to think, work out problems, understand plan and read, etc.;
   (c) to have time to write detailed reports for supervision;
   (d) also to have at least one case capable of movement in order to feel he has achieved something and can see results of his work.

2. *Process recordings*
   These are expected to play a large part in teaching in this placement, as they
   (a) show the student's development;
   (b) highlight student's areas of difficulty.

   It is useful if the student does at least one process recording on each client, in addition to process recording each interview in one specific case. The tutor will wish to see the process recordings, preferably before visiting the agency, in order to have an idea of the work the student is doing and his level of performance.

3. *Work with clients by the end of the first placement*
   (a) Ability to begin using the relationship to work on client's problems with awareness and sensitivity to

clients' reactions to situations.
(b) Awareness and understanding of the significance of non-verbal communication, though this may still come retrospectively.
(c) Ability to use the relationship to create a warm, sympathetic atmosphere to enable clients to explore uncomfortable areas, controlling any anxiety the student may feel; the beginning of development of ability to tolerate hostility though at this stage the student may not yet be able to use clients' negative feelings constructively; to work towards helping clients confront painful areas rather than maintain a 'cosy' relationship, i.e. the ability to tolerate and understand the negative transference phenomenon as well as the positive.
(d) Developing capacity to assess situations though significance may still be seen later, by collecting information and understanding what is relevant.
(e) Awareness that past experience contributes to clients' present reactions and handling of circumstances.
(f) The importance of including clients in the planning of goals and accepting dependency of clients with awareness that there must be limits.
(g) Understanding of the problems involved in the transfer or termination of cases.
(h) Ability to try out different social work methods.

4. *Organisation and functioning*
   (a) Good knowledge of social and allied professional services and resources.
   (b) Ability to record clearly and appropriately for agency and supervision.
   (c) Ability to work in a team.
   (d) Ability to organise own time efficiently.

5. *Development as a professional worker*
   (a) Ability to use supervision constructively.
   (b) Good preparation for supervision, e.g. process records handed in in time for supervisor to have read and commented on them before supervision session.

(c) Development of self-awareness, e.g. of own reactions to clients, though not necessarily yet the ability to cope with or use this.

(d) Beginnings of ability to relate theory to practice.

(e) Identification as a professional worker with awareness of the difference between a professional relationship and friendship with understanding of the reasons for this.

Final Placement

1. *Caseload*
This may be increased slightly, e.g. to 8, as student may be doing less process recordings and is finding it easier to write these which he is doing. He may also be taking on a number of short-term cases or be involved in intake work.

2. *Process recordings*
These are still useful as a teaching tool, and in demonstrating the development of the student's work. He should also be writing reports for other agencies, e.g. Court reports, social histories, etc.

3. *Work with clients*
All items mentioned in first placement should be developed further.

(a) Greater ability to assess situations quickly and decide which social work method is appropriate in terms of client's total life situation, personality, in addition to time and resources available.

(b) Ability to use the relationship and assessment to work on clients' problems.

(c) Awareness of his own part in the relationship and its effect on the client together with control of his own reactions.

(d) Ability to help the client confront painful areas and explore, with acceptance, those which client feels to be unacceptable.

(e) Understanding of client's right to his own opinions with the awareness of possible ethical problems where these conflict with student's or society's own.

(f)   Knowledge of where permissive approach is appropriate and where authority is necessary.

(g)   Ability to transfer or terminate a case with sensitivity and skill.

4. *Organisation and functioning*

(a)   Ability to record efficiently for agency and other professional agencies and services.

(b)   Ability to select priorities appropriately.

(c)   Greater initiative and confidence in decision making, with a sense of responsibility.

(d)   Ability to work in a flexible way within the agency structure.

5. *Development as a professional worker*

(a)   Ability to accept critically the agency policies and structure within which he works, but also to accept the client and his needs as an individual in society.

(b)   Ability to accept criticism but confidence to put forward his own ideas.

(c)   The capacity to relate theory to practice, with integration of the two.

(d)   Knowledge of the need for continued learning, the wish for this and the need for continued integration and consolidation.

Evaluation

It is useful for the supervisor to see any previous evaluation before the start of the placement, to help him ascertain

What stage the student has reached.

Special areas of strength and weakness, indicating areas for concentration of teaching.

How to offer a new experience to the student.

However, it is important for the supervisor not to prejudge the student; his assessment may not entirely agree with the previous supervisor's, and where this is so, it needs close examination to discover exactly what is happening.

Matching of student to supervisor is very important (see chapter 2) but sometimes this does go wrong and, as a result, unresolved personality difficulties can become reflected in a biased evaluation.

Student evaluation is continuous throughout the placement. It is important for the student to be aware of this and for student and supervisor both to be aware of the supervisor's power to pass or fail. It is always a cause of anxiety in the student who is expected to:

> expose all his weaker areas to the supervisor and to seek help with his difficulties; as well as having his work and his personality in relation to his work constantly criticised and assessed with a view to his passing or failing to qualify as a social worker.

This type of vulnerable situation where a usually mature person is felt to be infantilised and exposed, needs great skill in handling by the supervisor. It is essential to establish a relationship of trust as soon as possible and to discuss all these feelings openly.

The continuous assessment needs to be a joint exercise, between the supervisor and student; the student may need help in developing a realistic capacity for self-evaluation and in not over-emphasising either his strengths or his weaknesses.

Evaluation needs to be seen in a positive, developmental way, with strengths stressed in the written assessment as well as the areas needing further help.

The value of a written evaluation is that:

> it pin-points learning areas and focuses thinking;
> it can highlight areas needing further help, which the supervisor, student and tutor had all missed.

It is therefore very useful for there to be a mid-placement evaluation. If there is no official requirement for this by the college, the supervisor may find it extremely difficult to discipline himself into writing one, however much he recognises its value. When this is the case, the tutor's visit can be used as an opportunity to make a joint verbal evaluation by going through the outline in relation to the student. There is still time left in the placement, when this is done, to work on any problems which have been highlighted as a result.

Students should always be able to discuss their evaluations before they are written, as well as reading the final copy before it is sent to the college. In the case of a student violently disagreeing with the supervisor's written assessment, his own comments should be included at the end; in any event, both supervisor and student should sign the evaluation; the college then knows that it has been read by the student (see Butler and Elliott 1985).

Some supervisors avoid showing the student the final copy, though it has been seen in draft; this may be because of a reluctance to discuss openly areas which give cause for concern, and where the relationship between supervisor and student makes it difficult to deal with problem areas. If supervisory notes are kept as well as a practical work record, and everything is discussed freely as it emerges, then there should be no need for this type of situation to arise.

If the supervisory relationship has developed with trust and frankness, the written evaluation should hold nothing new for the student.

The Student Who Fails (see Davies 1979; Butler and Elliott 1985)
Students' reactions: Implicit in the concept of evaluation is the concept of possible failure. This can cause a variety of problems and anxieties in the student group, particularly if there is a question of failure amongst one of their number.

These anxieties are best dealt with (depending on the particular student and his group):

Openly, in college groups; or individually, where they need clarification and open discussion.

Individually in the placement as other supervisors' relationships with students are likely to be affected. The tutor and supervisor need to spell out constantly exactly where the student is seen to be in relation to passing and failing.

The possibility of failure is one of the reasons for some students' request that evaluations be abolished, arguing that as they were originally social workers before coming on the course, the question of pass or fail is irrelevant. The potential dangers to the client here are great, and it puts an onus on the person(s) selecting students for the course, never to make a mistake. However, if it is a qualifying course, students have to be assessed in order to qualify. Normally, they have to pass in both academic and practical fields, with various systems of referral, depending on the particular course.

Supervisor's position
The supervisor of a student with a possibility of failure in practical work needs constant college support throughout the placement.

The ultimate responsibility for failure should rest with the Examining Board. The supervisor should never be left to feel solely responsible.

Failure should be assessed on the basis of more than one placement where factors such as clashes of personality between supervisor and student may have been influential.

The supervisor and tutor should be in very close touch with each other.

The supervisor may have feelings of failure as a teacher and educator; he may need help from the tutor in confronting the student with the reality of possible failure.

In any question of failure, however much he feels for the student's position, it is important for the supervisor to remember that he is primarily responsible to the clients as well as to the agency, and that he must not risk damage to clients being incurred. If a student does fail, he also will need a great deal of counselling, help and support as well as advice as to what his future direction might be. Each situation varies as to who is the most appropriate person to give this help; it may be felt, after discussion between student, supervisor and tutor, that outside help is necessary.

Grading

The subject of grading may cause problems. Most courses nowadays do not ask the supervisor to grade the student's work, but all do need the supervisor to indicate very clearly whether, in his opinion, the student should gain distinction, pass, fail, or is borderline between any one of these. Some courses leave it at that, whereas others award a mark after discussion between tutor and supervisor, the final mark being verified at the examiners' meeting.

The reason for the supervisor not putting any mark on the written evaluation is that as the final mark is awarded only at the examiners' meeting, the student may have serious cause for complaint if it is altered, particularly if it is lowered.

The grading position should be clarified with the student who otherwise may become unduly anxious.

Evaluation Outlines

Most courses produce an outline, though some only indicate

areas they would like commented on, but leave it to the supervisor to use what framework, if any, he prefers.

Common features of all outlines considered to be essential are:

> Relationships established and sustained with clients and in the agency.
>
> Ability to make assessments.
>
> Ability to use assessments and relationships to work on clients' problems.
>
> Organisational abilities, e.g. use of time, recording, letter-writing, use of telephone.
>
> Use of supervision.
>
> Development as a professional person.

Below is an example of an evaluation outline mainly for fieldwork placements, and one for community and group-work placements.

(1)   OUTLINE FOR REPORT OF FIELDWORK PLACEMENTS

1. (a) Student's name, age.
   (b) Course: which placement (e.g. first or second) with dates.
   (c) Agency: name, address, brief description — e.g. agency function, number of staff, etc.
   (d) Supervisor (signature) — position held.
   (e) Date of report.

2. (a) Brief description of student and caseload indicating in each the problem; work achieved by the student; number of interviews over what period of time and whether home visits or office interviews.
   (b) Other activities engaged in during the placement (if this section is prepared by the student, this should be indicated).

3. *Work with clients*
   (a) *Relationships*
        Ability to establish, develop, sustain and terminate relationships; to use them to work on the client(s) problems, both internal and external; student's per-

ceptiveness and sensitivity to overt hidden feelings of client(s); ability to tolerate expression of client(s) feelings and to respond appropriately.
(b) *Ability to assess situations*
Ability to elicit relevant information; to understand the client(s) reactions; to understand the client(s) practical and emotional needs, powers of observation and listening; capacity for balanced judgement; ability to analyse a situation and to define with client(s) the problem areas; making realistic treatment plans with the client.
(c) *Ability to use assessment*
Capacity to implement the plan(s); ability to modify goal(s) in the light of changing knowledge and circumstances; capacity to make a realistic evaluation of work done.

4. *Organisation and functioning within the agency*
(a) Understanding the limits and functions of the agency; relationships established with colleagues and other agencies, and ability to work in a team setting.
(b) Administrative ability; ability to organise time and resources; punctuality, reliability; capacity for taking decisions; initiative and responsibility; appropriate use of other agencies and professional services; use of the telephone, etc.
(c) Recording: file reports; reports for other agencies; reports for supervision; letter-writing.

5. *Development as a professional worker*
(a) Use of supervision: relationship with supervisor and ability to use supervision to develop professional skills; attitude to learning.
(b) Development of self-awareness and of capacity to handle own feelings appropriately in the work situation.
(c) Ability to identify with a professional role and student's confidence in his capacity to give a social work service.

6. *Placement agreement*
How far the objectives set down in the placement agree-

ment have been fulfilled.

7. *Summary*
    (a) Areas in which progress has been made during the placement.
    (b) Areas for future development.
    (c) Any special strengths or weaknesses in the student's performance and personality, with any comments not already noted.
    (d) For final placements: whether the standard of performance reached by the student is what one would expect from a newly qualified social worker.

(2)   OUTLINE FOR THE ASSESSMENT OF STUDENTS ON COMMUNITY AND GROUP WORK PLACEMENTS

Note to Supervisors: Please select those points relevant to your agency and your particular student's project, as these guidelines are written to cover a wide range of group and community work placements.

1. *The agency*
    A brief description of the nature of the agency and the work done by it.

2. *The placement*
    Was the project engaged upon a new area of work or an existing project? What were the aims and expectations of student and supervisor of the placement? A description of the work done by the student and the outcome of the work.

3. *Assessment of student's abilities* and issues for further work and development.
    (i) Can the student plan and work through a project or piece of work? Can he/she define aims and stick to them?
    (ii) Can the student make appropriate interventions? How well did the student understand and use leadership and/or co-leadership and authority roles?
    (iii) Can student understand and use the group processes?

(iv) How well does he cope with aggression and challenge in a group? Can he cope with the unexpected?
(v)   How well has the student used supervision?
(vi) How well did the student work as part of a team,
and relate to colleagues?
(vii) How well has the student recorded for the agency
and for him/herself, and done administrative work?

4. *General comments*
Strengths and weaknesses and areas for further development and work. Recommendation for pass or fail.

Use of Written Evaluation

The evaluation is usually college property, though the student is given a copy.

There is cause for concern in some local authorities where
the practice is for the training officer to keep a copy of every
evaluation written in his social services department. There are
various reasons given for this, the most common one being
that it is his responsibility to ensure that adequate standards
are maintained by supervisors in his agency; this questions
the position of colleges and tutors, who presumably do not
use ineffective supervisors, and in any event, discuss their
reservations with the training officer concerned.

The written evaluation is an assessment of the student's
learning and professional skills at a particular point in time.
It is not a reference. The dangers of its circulating around
departments or of copies being kept by training officers are
great, and if the supervisor has any fears of this occurring, the
final written evaluation is likely to be less than honest. This
is unhelpful to the student, college and supervisor.

It is appropriate for all concerned to express anxiety at
the question of confidentiality of the evaluation if there is
a likelihood of a copy being kept in the training department's
files and possibly being used later as the basis for a reference.

Summary

Essential experience for students in all fieldwork placements:
History taking, assessment and intervention planning.
Discussion and decision-making with clients in shaping
goals, making transactions and contracts.

Dealing with practical problems which may reveal other problem areas for client.

Significance of the client/worker interaction.

Non-verbal communication in interviews.

Defence mechanisms and forms of manipulation.

Use of dependency in the client.

Use of transference and counter-transference phenomena.

Recording, letter-writing, etc.

The Case Study

An exercise in integration. The student may be required to do this as part of the assessment procedure. It is useful if one can be done during the first placement, as an early exercise in relating theory to practice, and a final, more extensive one at the end of the course. The case study should be on a client/clients the student is currently working with on the placement.

Outline examples follow.

GUIDE FOR A CASE STUDY (FIELDWORK)

1. Outline of case before referral to student. Social history.

2. Case looked at from all theories of different social work methods and intervention. Discuss different reasons for choosing particular method but also show how knowledge of all psychological theories helps in understanding the client and his problem.

3. Chronological development of social work intervention. Assessment and intervention plans showing the problem as identified by client and student. Assessment should include ego-strengths, motivation of client, etc:
    (i)   Include number and frequency and place of interviews.
    (ii) Content: verbal and non-verbal interaction.
    (iii) Relationship: including part social worker played and how he/she and client related to each other.

4. Movement throughout contact, including:
   - (a) how client and worker modified original assessment, focus, opinions, etc. with fresh knowledge;
   - (b) how relationship developed;
   - (c) how social worker adapted different techniques;
   - (d) what theoretical framework was used and why.

5. Summary and conclusions, including:
   - (a) work achieved;
   - (b) indications for future;
   - (c) how case was transferred or closed and client's reactions;
   - (d) how social worker helped client through these reactions;
   - (e) social worker's own feelings on leaving client.

GUIDE FOR CASE STUDY ON THERAPEUTIC GROUPWORK PLACEMENTS

Brief description of the agency and its service.
History of the group, your role if any, in its inception.
Aims of the group. Was there a contract?
Composition and size — how satisfactory were these in terms of group needs?
Brief description of group members and what brought them to the group.
What theories were helpful to you in the understanding of and participation in your group?

Analysis of the group processes during the period of your involvement. If possible identify group phases and relate these to the interventions of the worker(s). (Do not forget the termination phase or your own departure.)

Observe whether and how Programme, if any, furthered the aims of the group.

You could *either*:
(a) select a client and analyse his role in the group, his effect on and interaction with other members, his identification with or resistance to group task, and his relationship to

group workers. What in your view he derived from his group experience.

or

(b) take the whole group as your focus, analysing it as above, but more holistically. What themes emerged, group fears, defences, conflicts, resolutions? How did the group use individual members to express or deal with its preoccupations?

or

(c) if your setting was a Therapeutic Community you may take the community as your focus. Observe the relationship between its culture and its structure. Analyse the function of and relation between the various groups (large, small, sensitivity, etc.) and describe your own role and feelings in each.

Whichever approach you choose, select one or two group sessions to describe in some detail with a commentary, showing your understanding of group processes. Include an account of your development as a group worker/co-worker, the feelings aroused in you by the group, areas of difficulty and of growth.

GUIDE FOR CASE STUDY IN COMMUNITY WORK AND SOCIAL GROUPWORK

1. *Agency setting. History and background to the project*
   Who defined the need for the project; what were its original aims; what were the expectations by student and supervisor of the project?

2. *Theoretical concepts* or approaches in group or community work which were useful.

3. A *Description of the project* relating your description to theory where possible and bringing out your own interventions. The description might go through some or all of the following phases:

(i)   Planning.
(ii) Beginning the project or making contacts.
(iii) Setting up a group — establishing goals.
(iv) The group process and role of the worker.
(v)   Ending.
(vi) Evaluation.

Equally if a student is joining an existing project then a description of the work done might follow his or her beginning, middle and ending phases.

4. *Summary and conclusions* This section might include a discussion of the worker's role and comments on leadership; comments arising from any aspect of the work described in 3 above; theoretical issues arising from the work done; personal lessons learnt, and growth points or further developments recommended for the project.

8 Termination of Placement

Preparation for Termination

Paradoxically, planning for termination is an integral part of the overall planning of the placement.

There is often an inbuilt reluctance of the supervisor and the student to look at the termination of the placement and the problems it brings up; these are the clients' reactions, the student's and supervisor's reactions, those of the other workers in the agency, and the college. The issue of evaluation reaches its height of importance at the end of the placement but if it has been handled throughout the placement as suggested in chapter 7, it need not hold too many anxieties for the supervisor or student, as there should be nothing new in it.

Termination and/or Transfer of Student's Cases

Discussion of how to handle termination and transfer should take place between the student and supervisor when the student first takes on the case, as it is part of the assessment and treatment planning procedure.

If the student introduces himself to every client by telling him of the length of time they will be working together, the student automatically limits himself in his social work method to that of a time-limited contract. Not all clients can use this method, nor does it allow the student to gain experience in extended casework.

If the client knows of the worker's departure from the beginning, or early on in the relationship, the focus of work may be so much on termination, that other problems are left untouched.

When making assessment and planning appropriate methods of intervention, the supervisor and student also need to discuss how and when the client should be told of the student's leaving.

In open-ended casework, the optimum time for telling the client is about four weeks before the end of the placement, assuming that the client is being seen weekly. This allows time for him to express his reactions (see below) in a number of ways including failing to attend the subsequent interview. It also allows time for the social worker to help the client express his feelings and come to terms with them as well as taking a more realistic part in the decision as to whether or not he needs another social worker.

The student will have to decide, in conjunction with the supervisor, what reason to give the client for his leaving, and be aware of the possible effects of this (see below).

Transfer to another worker

If the decision is made to transfer the case to another worker, a number of issues immediately arise.

Frequently the student wishes for a particular social worker to take over the case, often his supervisor, whom he can trust to handle it well, but the social worker may be unwilling or unable to do so. The student may know that the client will not be followed up. He may only be able to tell him either to contact the office should a crisis occur, or that a social worker may be able to call at a later date. He may be unable even to give the name of the next social worker, who possibly has not yet been appointed to the agency. The difficulties and the feelings in the student, client and supervisor should be thoroughly acknowledged and explored in supervision; this will help the student to be sensitive to the client's reactions.

Where the student is lucky enough to be able to transfer the client to a worker before he leaves, it is useful if a joint interview can be arranged. There has been much debate as to the advisability of this, it being alleged that the student is unable to free himself from the client; that the client must go through the mourning work involved in termination before he can begin a relationship with another worker, etc. It should be remembered that the discussion is about social work students, and their clients, not psychoanalysts or psychotherapists. The client may need a bridge until a new relationship is formed. It helps if he has been given a name and can meet the person. Problems such as asking if he is allowed to keep in touch with the student, for example, by letter, need full discussion. It may be reassuring at the time if the client feels that he can, but if a new relationship is established quickly, he is unlikely to need this. Students justifiably fear that if clients wish to keep in touch it is not in their long-term interests, as it obstructs the relationship with the new worker. A resolution may be reached if the new worker acts as a bridge, in this way, by agreeing to let the student know how the client is. Once the transfer has been made, the student should cease to have contact with the client. He may need support from his supervisor in this.

Gifts

This is too large a subject to explore here, but the supervisor and student need to discuss it, not only in relation to termination. Questions such as what type of gift, from cups of tea to wedding presents; why the client needs to give; how often he gives, all need examination, in addition to when, how, why and what the student should or should not accept; limits of gift making and receiving need clarification.

Hospital placements offer a peculiar problem in termination, in that it is still possible for a student to discover that a client has been discharged in his absence and without his knowledge.

Transfer and termination summaries are not only useful to the agency and any future workers but an excellent way of evaluating what the student has achieved; they pull together the assessment, intervention plans, summarise the movement and indicate possible areas for future work, as well as areas untouched. It is a useful review of the work done in the placement and is usually included in the evaluation for the college.

Clients' Reactions

The student needs to be aware of the meanings of clients' reactions to his leaving. A few more common ones may be mentioned here.

The client may cease to engage in any further work.

He may use the knowledge as a spur to further rapid movement.

He may deny having any negative feelings about the worker's going, and make the student's job very hard in even allowing acknowledgement that such feelings are natural and to be expected.

With the denial, the client may express only very positive feelings towards the worker, in order to protect himself from his feelings of pain and yet another rejection.

The client who has already had a large number of social workers may feel he has a close enough relationship to the agency so as not to be unduly bothered by the student's leaving.

The client may not keep the next appointment, as already mentioned, or may fail to come again at all.

Covert and overt hostility may be expressed in a number of other ways.

The student needs guidance and understanding in order to help the client through this period.

Of course, if the work engaged in has been completed the client may feel happy and content at termination.

Student's Reactions

There will be guilt feelings about leaving clients with whom the work has not been finished. The current popularity of problem-centred brief casework may in part be due to a need to avoid guilt feelings surrounding the morality of using clients as teaching material. Feelings such as these plus availability and maximisation of community resources should not, ideally, influence the choice of social work method; choice should be made on the basis of assessment of the client's problem and his ability to use help.

The student may have anxieties about what happens to his clients after he has left, believing no-one else can be as concerned about them.

He is likely to have mixed feelings about leaving the agency; there may be some sadness in leaving his clients, supervisor and the other workers; his supervisor can help him with this in relating it to his clients' reactions and to the handling of mourning theory, generally. The feelings experienced can therefore be used by the supervisor to help him in his professional development.

The student may procrastinate in telling the client he is leaving; he may be seeking to choose the right moment, but such a moment never comes. The client always produces some minor crisis or emotional state and the student feels quite unable to be the cause of yet another blow. This may go on until the penultimate interview, when the student bursts out with it. Any hope of being able to help the client to deal with his leaving is then very small.

The student should be made aware that many clients

demonstrate a great deal of movement after the termination; it is a result of the work achieved, but the student is not there to see it. It can be very helpful if the supervisor subsequently informs the student when this occurs.

In situations where the student becomes a member of the agency staff at the end of his course, these feelings and problems may be avoided. It is questionable whether this is altogether in the interests of his long-term professional development if there has been only one placement on the course.

The student is likely to have anxieties surrounding his immediate future, whether it be another placement or becoming a qualified worker.

Supervisor's Reactions
The supervisor also has a variety of feelings at the end of the placement. He, too, may have anxieties about what is happening to the clients and whether or not they can be transferred to other workers.

He may experience feelings of sorrow that the student is leaving, or be welcoming a well-needed break from supervision.

There is a danger of his having 'killed off' the student before the end of the placement, particularly if he is to take another student and is already preparing for the next placement. The student will then feel the loss of interest acutely. The supervisor needs to stay with the student and be concerned about his immediate future, whether it is that the student has anxieties about a new placement, or about becoming qualified (see above).

The supervisor's feelings about being part of the teaching team need acknowledging by the college; if he is not to take another student, he may feel useless and rejected, as well as having been used and discarded by the college.

The supervisor will be very satisfied with the progress of a good student, but will need a great deal of support from the college throughout the placement, particularly in the evaluating stage, if there is a question of failure (see Butler and Elliott 1985).

Some Other Specific Problems
Some problems have already been mentioned in the previous sections of this chapter. Whichever the placement, whether

it is a first or final one, it is important to see its end in the context of a continuing professional development.

With a first placement, there may be a problem analogous to that of the student's leaving the client, namely, a desire to perpetuate the relationship; the student may wish to return to see the supervisor and agency, but this may not be helpful in his next placement, particularly if both supervisor and agency differ in approach and attitudes. Not only will he then be in danger of splitting college and field, but the placements and supervisors may be similarly split. This problem should be discussed openly between the tutor, supervisors and student, should it occur.

The end of the final placement coincides often with the end of the whole course. The student then has feelings about leaving not only the agency, but the college and the group of students. He has anxieties about his ability to function adequately as a qualified worker. He is concerned about the quality of future supervision and support. He usually feels ill-equipped and untrained, knowing that he is likely to be expected to know everything as a qualified worker, and to be far more skilled than he is. Expectations of newly qualified workers are more realistic than they used to be; nevertheless students have a genuine cause for anxiety.

It is helpful at the end of the course if the supervisor and student discuss the possibility of future contact for support and consultation. The student may also wish to use the college tutor for this.

Students need to be told that they will not be aware of how much they have learned on the course and internalised until much later. A period for integration and consolidation is necessary after the end of the course, with supervision and a limited caseload, if the greatest use is to be made of their training and educational experience.

AUTHOR'S NOTE

This book is no substitute for a supervisors' training course, nor is it a substitute for discussions and seminars on supervision. However, it can be used in conjunction with these, and in situations where a social worker finds himself supervising without access to such aids it should be a useful guide.

References

Barclay Report (1982), *Social Workers: Their Role and Tasks*, London: Bedford Square Press.

BASW Publications (1983), *Effective and Ethical Recording*, Birmingham: BASW.

Brandon, J. and Davies, M. (1979), 'The limits of competence in social work: The assessment of marginal students in social work education', *British Journal of Education for Social Work*, 9(3), pp. 295—347.

Briscoe, C. and Thomas, D. (ed.) (1977), *Community Work: Learning and Supervision*, National Institute of Social Services Library, No. 32, London: Allen and Unwin.

Butler, B. and Elliott, D. (1985), *Teaching and Learning for Practice*, Community Care Practice Handbooks, Aldershot: Gower.

Butrym, Z.T. (1976), *The Nature of Social Work*, London: Macmillan.

CCETSW (1981), *Revised Guidelines* (Supplement to Paper 15: (1977) *Guidelines for Courses Leading to the CQSW*), London: Central Council for Education and Training in Social Work.

Cross, C. (ed.) (1974), *Interviewing and Communication in Social Work*, London: Routledge and Kegan Paul.

Davies, M. (1979), 'Fieldwork failures — a very rare breed', *Community Care*, 282, pp. 16—18.

Davies, M. (1985), *The Essential Social Worker*, 2nd edn, Aldershot: Gower.

DHSS (1983), Local Authority Circular: *Personal Social Services Records: Disclosure of Information to Clients*, LAC(83)14.

Dwyer, M. and Urbanowski, M. (1965), 'Student process recording: A plea for structure', *Social Casework*, 46, p. 5.

Garrett, A. (1972), *Interviewing, its Principles and Methods*, FSAA.

Goldstein, H. (1973), *Social Work Practice: A Unitary Approach*, University of South Carolina Press.

Harris, R.J. (1983), 'Social Work Education and the transfer of learning', *Issues in Social Work Education*, 3(2), pp. 103—17.

Hollis, F. (1964), *Casework: A Psychosocial Therapy*, New York: Random House.

Kadushin, A. (1976), *The Social Work Interview*, New York: Columbia University Press.

Kaslow and Associates (1977), *Supervision, Consultation and Staff Training in the Helping Professions*, London: Jossey-Bass.

Keith-Lucas, A. (1972), *Giving and Taking Help*, University of North Carolina Press.

Kent, B. (1969), *Social Work Supervision in Practice*, Oxford: Pergamon Press.

Martel, S. (ed.) (1981), *Supervision and Team Support: Social Work Practice in FSU*, London: Bedford Square Press.

Mattinson, J. (1975), *The Reflection Process in Casework Supervision*, London: IMS.

Olson, U.J. and Pegg, P.F. (1979), 'Direct open supervision: a team approach', *Family Process*, 18, pp. 463—9.

Øvretveit, J. (1985), *Client Access and Social Work Recording*, BIOSS: Brunel University.

Payne, C. and Scott, T. (1982), *Developing Supervision of Teams in Field and Residential Social Work*, Paper No.12, NISW.

Perlman, H.H. (1957), *Social Casework: A Problem-Solving Process*, Chicago: University of Chicago Press.

Pettes, D.E. (1979), *Staff and Student Supervision: A Task-centred Approach*, National Institute of Social Services Library, no.34, London: Allen and Unwin.

Pincus, A. and Minahan, A. (1973), *Social Work Practice: Model and Method*, F.E.Peacock.

Probert, N. (1985), 'Client access to records in social work', London: RHBNC, M.Sc. extended essay (unpublished).

Rapoport, L. (1970), 'Crisis intervention as a mode of treatment', Roberts and Nee (eds) (1970), *Theories of Social Casework*, Chicago: University of Chicago Press.

Reid, J.W. and Epstein, L. (1972), *Task Centred Casework*, New York: Columbia University Press.

Smalley, R. (1967), *Theory for Social Work Practice*, New York: Columbia University Press.

Star, B. (1979), 'Exploring the boundaries of video-tape self-confrontation', *Journal of Education for Social Work*, 15(1), pp. 87—94.

Stephens, J.M. (1963), 'Transfer of learning' in Grose, R.F. and Birney, R.C. (eds) (1963), *Transfer of Learning*, New York: Van Nostrand.

Westheimer, I.J. (1977), *The Practice of Supervision in Social Work*, London: Ward Lock Educational.

Wijnberg, M.H. and Schwartz, M.C. (1977), 'Models of student supervision: The Apprentice, growth and role systems models', *Journal of Education for Social Work*, 13(3), pp. 107—13.

Young, P. (1967), *The Student and Supervision in Social Work Education*, London: Routledge and Kegan Paul.

Young, P. (1979), 'Social work training: seeing it the CCETSW way', *Community Care*, 290, pp. 26—7.

Index